ANTHRACITE BOOT CAMP

Louis Ronald Scatena

This story is about my Father, Pete Scatena, and anthracite coal mining. It is also dedicated to my Mother, Caroline, who to this day at age 98, never waivers in her devotion to her principles. By example, and with a subtle pride based on her own personal unwritten code, she taught Linda, Carol, and I the true meaning of "**HONOR**" under any circumstances of personal hardship. In the context of her life, Honor is defined as, "Always taking the path in support of family, friends, and country, as God intended, and without any deviation in that path for personal gain." This story is Mother's, as much as it is Dad's.

ANTHRACITE BOOT CAMP

Louis Ronald Scatena

ISBN (Print Edition): 978-1-09834-943-1

ISBN (eBook Edition): 978-1-09833-053-8

TABLE OF CONTENTS

PREFACE

This is a true story about men struggling in a black underground world as they and their families emerge from a very difficult period of industrial labor unrest and civil economic depression. It is also a story of a father's effort to train his young son to work with the degree of diligence and intensity that the father felt was the necessary foundation for a successful and rewarding life. This story is not about coal mining in the coal veins where those seams are deep, thick, and overlain by many feet of solid rock. It is not about miners at major coal collieries who rode on cable cars down a shaft or slope, and stood erect in high underground, well-lit mine chambers. In other words, it's not about underground labor as was often portrayed in such classic films about coal mining as "*How Green Was My Valley*", "*The Molly Maguires*", or on public television. Certainly, those miners persevered in a monumentally hazardous environment that is well documented, and their contributions to the formation of an organized Miners' Labor Union were heroic, indeed.

Instead, this story is about anthracite mining along the mountainsides where the coal seams slant upward to the surface—i.e., in mining terms, where the veins "outcrop". Here coal veins and roof rock above the veins are thin, and roof rock more often than not, is extensively fractured and ready to collapse. Coal veins may only be three to five feet thick, dip, turn, twist, abruptly terminate, resume a short distance away, and often cannot be identified accurately by the official names of veins in the library of anthracite mine maps. In such a confined layout, air ventilation is also poor. All of the safety issues that confronted miners in the large collieries were multiplied at these mines near the vein outcrops. State and Federal mine inspectors also visited these small operations, but most likely, not with the frequency and enthusiasm focused on larger collieries where the majority of anthracite miners were at risk. For all of these reasons, miners commonly nicknamed these small mine openings that once dotted the mountainsides of the anthracite coal fields as "dog-holes". Classic stories about coal mines tell of helpful warnings a swarm of rats provided by squealing as they frantically ran out of a mine just prior to a cave-in that they sensed was imminent. During my youthful experience around dog-holes from 1951 to 1959, I never heard that any rats were seen. It's likely that there weren't enough lunch bags around to sustain them. It's also possible the rats took one frightened look at the ominous dungeons and decided to migrate and break into miners' lunches elsewhere.

This story is also about my "boot camp" training from the age of nine to seventeen, in anthracite mining operations under the guidance of my Father, Pete Scatena. It took place in Northeastern Pennsylvania—specifically, the region between Scranton and Wilkes-Barre known as The Wyoming Valley. Most of the history of The Wyoming Valley is rooted in its' coal mining industry, which was the Valley's principal attraction for mass immigration by impoverished families from Europe in the late nineteenth and early twentieth centuries. A portion of the Valley appears in Figure 1. My personal experiences in this story occurred within a three-mile radius of the City of Pittston. Pittston appears in the upper left corner of the map, and is midway between the much larger cities of Scranton and Wilkes-Barre.

The story begins in Chapters 1 and 2 with a description of the strife and hardship that prevailed in anthracite coal fields at the time immigration was at its peak; i.e. 1878 to 1915. Chapter 3 describes the typical family struggles for survival subsequent to immigration, before and during the Great Depression; i.e. 1916 to 1939. It is only with an understanding of previous family hardship that one can accurately judge the sometimes odd and questionable motives of the generation of anthracite miners that followed after 1940, in Chapters 4 through 11. Knowledge of those earlier hardships certainly helped me to understand the subsequent motives of my hard-working Father, his parents, and the dog-hole miners who are the primary subject in this account of life around the mines. As you read, it is likely you will feel some of their actions were in-excusable; however, it would be grossly misleading and unfair to judge their actions, at that time, solely in the context of life as we now experience it today. However, some readers may be able to draw comparisons between the civil unrest of that period, and the current nature of our society in the year 2020. Chapter 12 ends with my departure from "Anthracite Boot Camp" in 1959, and to the beginning of U.S. Marine Corps Boot Camp. The chapter is also quite sad as it recalls a number of mine disasters and tragedies. The final "Epilogue" summarizes the Anthracite Boot Camp "Lessons Learned" that greatly enriched my subsequent personal life. It also describes how the experience inspired my on-going public service in Arizona as a Professional Structural Engineer, with fifty-five years of design, construction, and corporate experience, and hopefully, with many more years to come.

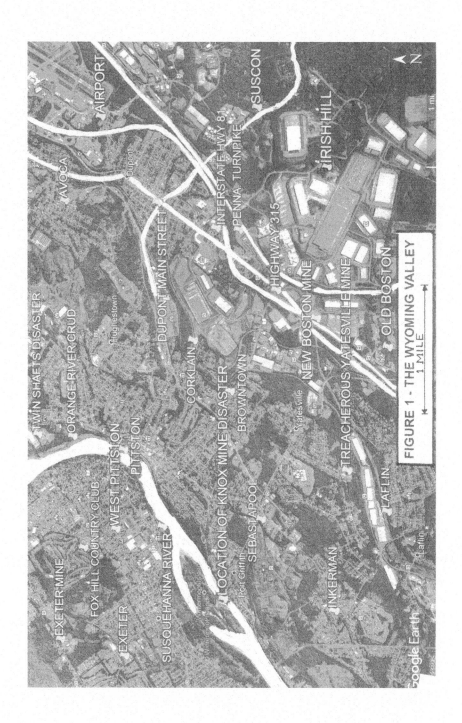

FIGURE 1 - THE WYOMING VALLEY

CHAPTER I

THE ANTHRACITE REVOLUTION (1878–1915)

This chapter is intended as background to provide an insight to the evolution and up-bringing of the miners, and the motives for their aggressive actions described later in this story. Around 1900, there were approximately 150,000 miners in the anthracite coalfields centered in the general vicinity of the Northeastern Pennsylvania cities of Scranton, Wilkes-Barre, Hazleton, and Pottsville. The production of anthracite not only fueled homes, but just as importantly, fueled the development of the steel, railroad, shipping, and other related industries to the point where the United States began to surpass Great Britain as the industrial capital of the world. But the wealth was accumulated by powerful industrialists at the expense of emigrants from Europe who sacrificed their sweat, tears, and blood after they read the glamorous and enticing advertisements (by the industrialists) of the rewards awaiting them in America. Compared to the famine that existed in their own native country, they were induced to beg and borrow the money needed to cover the cost of emigration. Once here, however, the miners soon realized that their participation in that "wealth" was only imagined. Industrialists created a network of six railroads in the northeastern United States in a concerted effort to control anthracite sales, prices, and wages. They also rejected and publicized union members as "De-stabilizing Socialists". Miners fought to establish unions that could support better wages and regulate safer mining conditions. On June 28, 1896 in Pittston, fifty-eight men and boys died 434 feet below ground in the Twin Shafts Disaster. None of their bodies were ever recovered, and thirty-one widows and 101 orphans were left behind. It was one of the largest of the many coal mining disasters in Pennsylvania history. A subsequent investigation demonstrated that mine safety standards were inadequate. The location of the disaster is shown at the top of Figure 1.

In addition to safer working conditions, miners fought for better wages. As the owners of the steel plants, railroads, banks, and other industries planned it, an annual income of 400-500 dollars was just enough to put bread and potatoes on a miner's plate to sustain his return to the colliery each day. Miners and their families often lived in shacks adjacent to the colliery and paid rent for the shacks to the mine operators. Mothers shopped at the company store where they were forced to pay the high prices because it was the only shop where they could buy on credit, as long as their underpaid husbands continued to mine coal. Tennessee Ernie Ford summed up the miners' sorrowful predicament in his 1955 hit song, "Sixteen Tons," when he sang, "*Saint Peter don't you take me cause I can't go. I owe my soul to the company store.*"

The movie titled "THE MOLLY MAGUIRES" was filmed in 1970 and is another excellent description of the hardships of miners and their families in the vicinity of Hazleton, which is slightly south of Wilkes Barre. However, this clandestine group for which the movie was titled, occasionally resorted to violence and espionage in attempts to resolve their disagreement with mine owners. In December of 1878, their principal leaders were identified, tried in court, and hanged. The movie was filmed just east of Hazleton at the Eckley Miner's Village, which once truly was a company-run village for miners and their families, and now is an anthracite museum. The role of the leader of "The Mollies", Jack Kehoe, was portrayed by the very popular Hollywood actor, Sean Connery. Yes, it is clear that Jack Kehoe was overly exuberant in his effort to help free miners from civil oppression; but it is also clear that he was devoted to a heroic and just cause, and not his personal well-being or profit. Throughout history, only a handful of heroic figures have displayed such total allegiance to the honor of mankind, with very little interest in personal gain. Remarkably in 1979, after a review of the case and a new understanding of how the industrialists organized the trial to their advantage, the Governor of Pennsylvania granted a pardon to Jack Kehoe, one-hundred years after "Black Jack" had been hanged in Pottsville.

In 1897, after dissolution of "The Mollies", a large group of miners peacefully demonstrated near Hazleton, and nineteen were shot and killed by a so-called "industry security force" in what has been historically recorded as the "Lattimer Massacre". After 1900, mine owners, industrialists, and their railroad subsidiaries continued to keep unions out, and had little regard for mine safety. On average, one anthracite miner was killed in a mine accident every day. In 1901, a total of five hundred and thirteen anthracite miners were killed and more than ten thousand seriously injured. Nevertheless, industrialists continued to hire private security forces to help control miners who demonstrated for fair wages and improvements to mine safety standards.

A series of prolonged, peaceful strikes by anthracite miners between 1900 and 1902 resulted in a national fuel crisis during which President Theodore Roosevelt created an Arbitration Commission. The Commission began to listen to testimony by miners and mine operators at the Lackawanna County Courthouse in Scranton in November, 1902. President Roosevelt hired the renowned socialist lawyer, Clarence Darrow, to facilitate testimony by miners for about six weeks, and John Mitchell of the fledgling United Mine Workers Union was interviewed for 5 days. In January and February of 1903, owners testified and accused demonstrating miners of destroying mine property and attacking "scabs", which was the miners' nickname for the 20,000 destitute miners who continued to work during the strike. In March of 1903, the Presidential Commission ruled that wages must be increased 10 percent, the wage must be based on each ton mined, the coal must be weighed fairly, and wages should rise as coal prices increase. President Roosevelt was sincere in his effort to help the miners; but he was also compelled to revive the seriously impacted steel and manufacturing industry from the coal strike that had crippled the nation. Therefore, the Commission also ruled that miners must return to work.

Despite the efforts of the President's Commission, the gains won by the fledgling United Mine Workers Union under John Mitchell, and the eloquent rhetoric of Clarence Darrow, only partial improvement occurred. If a miner received a net pay of ten dollars per week previously, he now received eleven, and the company store would likely find a way to recover all or part of the additional dollar. The plight of the anthracite miners would continue for thirty to thirty-five years as the United Mine Workers Union under John L. Lewis fought to gradually induce and implement safer working conditions, in addition to fair wage, health, and retirement programs. After 1902, the strike's most significant benefit was that for the first time, the miners now had a recognized voice in the American labor industry. However, miners across the country and around the globe continued their struggle for civil rights.

My grandfather Louis Scatena, (Nonno) immigrated to that difficult environment from Spoleto in North Central Italy in 1908, where he and his father, Bernardino, had worked in the lignite coal mines. Nonno was born in 1884. He and his father, Bernardino, were two of 800 to 900 men who worked in the large, state-of-the-art lignite coal mines in Morgnano, just outside the larger city of Spoleto, Italy. Lignite contains less carbon and produces less fuel than bituminous or anthracite. Nevertheless, the lignite was used to fuel the foundries in the larger industrial city of Terni, eighteen miles to the south of Spoleto. The mines opened in 1880 and here also, miners were under the oppressive control of industrialists based in Terni. Almost as if they had taken their cue from fellow miners in Northeastern Pennsylvania, the miners in Spoleto went on prolonged strikes in 1906 and 1907 to protest very dangerous working conditions and low wages. In 1907, the newspaper Giovanne Umbria wrote that Terni industrialists agreed to augment salary, *"Ma non a tutti, a chi merita,"* which literally translated said, *"But not for every miner; only those who merit it."* The League of Miners responded, *"This plan is unacceptable because it will create favoritism, jealousy, and discontent."* The newspaper also wrote, *"This plan is a delusion and is unsatisfactory. Now begins a period of severe confrontation."*

The Industrial Revolution was now underway at that time through-out coal mines, factories, and labor camps in many parts of the world. Nonno obviously hoped to participate in the wealth of anthracite mining at a colliery near the town of Plains, just north of Wilkes-Barre. Years ago, I had heard how Nonno, who died the year before I was born, was a staunch supporter of the Mine Worker's Union in The Wyoming Valley, and why he often found it necessary to carry a pistol and/or blackjack to defend himself during periods of labor unrest. My Father-in-Law, Peter Giovannini, was born in 1912 in Walsenburg, Colorado, where his father worked in the bituminous coal mines after the family had emigrated from Italy in 1911. However,

Pete's family returned to Italy in 1914 shortly after twenty-five people, including eleven children of striking coal miners, were killed by coal company guards and the Colorado National Guard in what history records as the "Ludlow Massacre". The guards were unaware that miners' wives and children were hiding in the waste disposal space under the tent platform when the guards set fire to the families' tents. Pete subsequently returned to America from Scheggia in North Central Italy in 1928 at age sixteen to work in an anthracite colliery near Jessup, Pennsylvania, just north of Scranton. Many years later, Pete described to me how he disembarked with tears of happiness at Ellis Island in 1928. He recalled how the ship's public address system softly distributed the very sentimental music of "La Vien Rose", as immigrants descended ramps to the pier. "Big Pete", as fellow miners called him, sadly recounted the grave conditions that he soon encountered in the anthracite coal mines, and his many battles with mine owners and scabs. Just like Nonno, he, too, was a staunch, outspoken member of the Mine Workers' Union. Unable to afford anything more sophisticated at that time, he described how bricks could be thrown far and accurately after banging two together to form smaller baseball-sized missiles. So despondent had Pete become over labor strife, poor pay, and hazardous mine conditions, he considered returning to Italy in 1929; however he couldn't, due to the stark realization that his parents had committed all of their financial resources to send him to America.

Twenty-five years after immigration, however, Big Pete had gradually worked his way up to a position of partnership in one of the largest and most productive mines in Scranton - The Diamond Colliery. From 1900 to 1940, however, such success was hardly a dream among anthracite miners.

CHAPTER II

IMMIGRATION AND ARRANGED
MARRIAGES (1905–1915)

Dad's mother, Nonna Ersilia Stella, was married to another miner before she married Nonno, and before Dad was born. Around 1913, Nonna's first husband, Luigi (Louis) Corsaletti, emigrated from Pastina, Italy, to work in an anthracite coal colliery in the Old Boston Mining Settlement, which is north of Wilkes-Barre. Pastina is a small farming village near the City of Gualdo. Nonna Ersilia and her three children - Uncle Ted, Aunt Della, and Aunt Vienna - remained behind in Pastina until such time as her first husband was financially able to send for them. Old Boston is approximately eight miles north of Wilkes-Barre, on the east side of State Highway 315 (Near bottom of Figure 1). As with most small towns in The Wyoming Valley, the origin of the settlement began with the construction of a nearby coal colliery in the Nineteenth Century, surrounded by the subsequent construction of shacks for the miners and their families. Louis Corsaletti's plan was obviously on track in 1914 because by then, he had purchased a small shack on Old Boston Road, about 1.5 miles from its' intersection at Highway 315. The shack was adjacent to the Old Boston Italian-American Citizen's Club. The club was demolished in 2019; but I have fond memories of the many evenings Dad took me there during my childhood to observe the miners playing bocce, darts, shuffleboard, card games, and the very vocal game of "Morra". The most exciting events occurred when the bocce team played other miners from similar clubs in Plains, Hudson, Keystone, Browntown, and other nearby anthracite mining villages, in an organized Bocce League. My unforgettable memories of the miners' very emotional outbursts during the games of "Bocce" and "Morra" will be described in an upcoming chapter.

The 1915 Wilkes-Barre Record Almanac reports that there were fourteen homicides in Luzerne County, Pennsylvania, in 1914. Although his "alleged indiscretion" was later disproved, it said of Nonna's first husband, *"In November, Luigi Corsaletti of Boston Settlement was shot by a boarding house keeper for alleged intimacy with the latter's wife."* A newspaper clipping from 1914 reported that the shooter *"claimed self-defense when Luigi drew a pistol first"*. The incident further testifies to the guns and lawlessness that existed in coal mining towns during that period. With the encouragement of her sister, Adele, who had already immigrated to the nearby town of Plains, Nonna, Uncle Ted Corsaletti, and Aunt Vienna immigrated to Old Boston in 1915 to live in the wood shack left by Nonna's deceased first husband. Aunt Della was left behind in Gualdo to live with Nonna's mother because Nonna felt it would be impossible to safely manage one baby and two small children during the long voyage. Nonna's sister, Adele, also wrote that Nonna would have a wonderful opportunity to wed a very nice, hardworking miner who was a personal friend to Adele and Adele's husband, Nazzareno Berrettini. Of course, the very nice man Adele was referring to was my Grandfather, "Nonno" Luigi (Louis) Scatena, who at the time, was rooming in a boarding house on Hilldale Avenue in the mining community of Plains. For many years, Adele's description of Nonno as "**NICE**" was hotly debated by his family after his death in 1941; but more about that hot debate later.

The following summary of Nonno's European background in coal mining is quite relevant to my story about anthracite mines. According to immigration records that I found available in the vast genealogical libraries of the Mormon Church in Salt Lake City, Luigi Scatena departed Naples, Italy, on August 29, 1908, on the SS CRETIC and arrived at Ellis Island in New York on September 11. In the ship's manifest, Nonno reported that he was twenty-four years old, single, could read/write, and had $24 in his possession. After seeing the quality of his personal signature on a "Petition for Naturalization" dated September 17, 1917, it raised a question in my mind whether Nonno could indeed 'write'. In one column of the ship's manifest, each immigrant had to report his occupation. On line after line, page after page, men responded: "**Laborer**," but Nonno responded: "**Miner**." It clearly suggested to me that Nonno and other coal miners were proud to make that distinction. In fact, it has dawned on me in recent years that I, too, feel proud to point to that distinctive coal mining experience and connection in my background. I can well understand why countless exhausted coal mines have been turned into visitor museums by municipalities world-wide. An historical account titled "*Le Miniere di Lignite di Spoleto*" by Giovanni Antonelli stated that the League of Miners near Spoleto, Italy was a proud fraternity. A literal translation of the preface states that "*the miners were an unusual hard-working breed, with strength and character, and born with a resolve to endure hardship*". The book's author also writes that the proud League hired artists to fabricate bronze statues of their leaders and heroes throughout the coal fields, and to design a colorful organizational flag. They also designated a special holiday called the Feast of Saint Barbara. The League celebrated the Feast and their Patron Saint each year in Spoleto with a very large festival on December 4. (2) Typically, Saint Barbara was worshipped by tradesmen who faced the danger of sudden and violent death in their work.

The miners of Northeastern Pennsylvania brought this strong sense of honor and pride with them from Europe, and passed it on to their descendants. Indeed, the fraternity of miners of Northeastern Pennsylvania celebrated John Mitchell Day on October 29. Many miners also looked forward to the annual "John Kehoe Celebration" at that coal magnate's estate in Harding, just up the Susquehanna River, a few miles north of Pittston. To what extent John Kehoe of the Twentieth Century was related to Jack Kehoe of the Molly Maguires in the Nineteenth Century, is uncertain. Unlike "Black Jack" Kehoe who was hung many decades earlier, John Kehoe owned collieries and breakers in The Wyoming Valley, and his estate on the bank of the Susquehanna River was magnificent. With pride in its coal mining history, the City of Scranton invites visitors to its' Anthracite Museum in West Scranton. Anthracite mining museums also exist near Hazleton, Pottsville, and other locations in Northeastern Pennsylvania. With similar pride, a museum has also been dedicated to the lignite miners at the shaft where Nonno and his father once worked in the small village of Morgnano, just outside Spoleto. The people, pride, perseverance, and politics of miners in Europe and Northeastern Pennsylvania were the same, separated only by several thousand miles of ocean.

The following is an intense description of Nonna Corsalletti's first meeting with Nonno Scatena in 1915 in the mining settlement of Old Boston. It was described to me in the following details by Aunt Della in 1987, many years after Nonna had recalled it for my Aunt.

"When Nonna entered the room where she knew she was about to meet her new husband for the first time, more than a dozen miners were seated against the walls around the room in their best Sunday outfits.

Very self-conscious and extremely nervous, with her head down, Nonna glanced around the room and out of the corner of her eye, one man, in particular, caught her attention. Nonna recalled that he had a robust, healthy complexion, well-groomed mustache, and a meticulous black suit, vest, and tie.

His trousers were tucked in wide leather straps that wrapped the top of his shining black boots. Nonna avoided eye contact with him and recalled telling herself, "*No, it can't be. I'm not that lucky!*" Nonna also sensed out of the corner of her eye, the miner was very intensely eying her up and down, and observing her every move. Then, as the other well-groomed miners seated against the walls passed a wine jug from one miner to the next, the man next to Nonno asked him if he wanted a drink, referring to him by Nonno Scatena's nickname: '*SCA-TAY' ! BEVE VINO, SCA-TAY'?* At that instant, Nonna said she lost her breath and recalled that Nonno replied, "*NO GRACI,*" and passed the wine jug to the man on his other side, without taking his glaring eyes off Nonna.

Immigrant miners typically had a strong preference to marry a woman from their native country. Nonna's somewhat "steamy account" is only one example of the many transatlantic arranged marriages of that period, and the circumstances leading to the next generation of anthracite miners. On my Mother's side of our family, my Grandmother Maria's marriage was also pre-arranged in a similar way by her brother, Michael Trombetta. After emigrating from Italy to Pittston in 1905, Grandmother Maria Trombetta and her Mother had been living with Mike and his family for some time on Parsonage Street in Pittston. Then one day, her brother angrily demanded that his sister, Maria, must **"GET A HUSBAND!"** In response to newspaper ads that Mike had placed, she interviewed and rejected one applicant after the other. Finally, her impatient brother demanded, **"THAT'S IT! YOU'RE MARRYING THE NEXT ONE THAT COMES THROUGH THAT DOOR!"**.........and of course, the next one through the door was my Mother's father, Nicholo Vigilante. If Mike were alive, I would buy him a bottle of Jack Daniels every Christmas!

The photo taken of Nicholo, Maria, and Maria's mother at, or shortly after their initial meeting 114 years ago, is very interesting. With one hand on his hip and the other holding a cigar, my Grandfather's stoic facial expression suggests the event may have been a 'business meeting'. Grandmother Maria appears very frightened, and her mother appears stern and upset. However, I have noticed that no one ever seemed to smile in any photos taken during those years. It was probably 'a sign of the time'. I have always had a profound appreciation for interpretive music, and enjoy using it to sum up memorable events, such as my grandparents' initial meetings prior to their arranged marriages. My sense is that Grandfather Nicholo Vigilante conducted himself very diplomatically in the initial meeting with Grandmother Maria, much in the style of Mario Lanza's very tender love ballad in 1952 titled, *"BECAUSE"*. In Nonno Scatena's case, however, his initial meeting with Nonna reminds me of Mario Lanza's smash hit and 'dynamic mandate' in 1950 titled, *"BE MY LOVE!"*

In the case of my Grandmother Maria Trombetta Vigilante, the subsequent 50 years of marriage proved to be ideal for the entire family. Grandfather Nicholo was an artistic and meticulous stone mason whose quality service was always in demand, though the demand was substantially reduced during the Great Depression. On the rare occasions someone needed a little masonry work during that tough economic period, he was the stone mason they turned to. It's probably a lesson in quality customer service that contractors should take note even today, as the current era of prosperity is not likely to endure forever. On the other hand, as with many other immigrants of that period, Nonna Ersilia would soon feel that her "luck" with her arranged marriage to Nonno Scatena may have been pre-maturely imagined. In retrospect, the behavioral differences between an artistic stone mason and a battling anthracite coal miner could have been somewhat predictable.

CHAPTER III

DESPERATION AND THE GREAT
DEPRESSION (1916–1939)

This chapter describes how miners not only fought for survival
underground, but also for the survival of their impoverished
families. Few people today can recall the extreme economic hardship
of that time, and I sometimes wonder if we shouldn't prepare for a
similar severe economic catastrophe that may someday return. To
begin, I recall that many years ago during one of my visits with her in
Hughestown, Aunt Della described for me how she cried in 1915 at
age four as she watched her mother, brother Dorato (Uncle Ted), and
sister, Aunt Vienna, ride away in horse and buggy to the train station.
She desperately reached for the rear of the buggy as tearful relatives
restrained her. Aunt Della said she refused to eat for many days and
became ill. It may seem a little odd that Aunt Della could remember
so many details from the age of four, and it may be possible that she
was recounting details shared over time by older relatives. However, I
can imagine that observing mother, sister, and brother saying good-
bye to everyone, and leaving home with suitcases, but without her,
could create an everlasting nightmare for a young girl, at any age. It
was not until 1922 at age eleven that Nonna and Nonno would send
for her. Aunt Della traveled to America from Italy with her aunt, who

was also immigrating to re-join her own coal mining husband near Pittston. After re-joining her family in Old Boston, Aunt Della said life was so hard, even six or seven years prior to the onset of the Great Depression, that she wished she could return to her grandmother in Italy. She said she felt, at that time, that the primary reason she had been summoned from Italy was to assist Nonna with housework, and to look after her younger sisters and brothers. "At that time" are the key words here because Aunt Della (and I) sincerely doubted this was Nonna's true motive. By this time, however, Nonna now had seven children to care for, in addition to a vegetable garden, chickens, pigs, bread-baking, and coal-picking for heating and baking. So great was the demand for Aunt Della's domestic service, Nonno refused to let her go to elementary school. When the truant officer paid a visit, Nonno would give him a few glasses of homemade red wine, a gallon of the freshly squeezed variety to take home, and an emotional plea that the household was enduring too much hardship to spare Aunt Della for elementary school. Nonna's dilemma at the time can only be imagined. In addition to the seven children already born between 1910 and 1922, she also endured the birth of three more children between 1922 and 1930. However, through seldom spoken innuendo, I learned that in addition to the birth of ten, Nonna also aborted four other pregnancies. Apparently, during the Depression, some forlorn women reverted to a painful method involving extremely hot bathwater soon after conception. According to information on the internet, this practice wasn't uncommon at that time, and was intended to aggravate the internal membranes to spontaneously induce abortion. Those who haven't heard of this very difficult period of time in our history will likely conclude such abortions were in-excusable. However, I distinctly recall Nonna's tenderness toward her ten children, or *"My chill-ee"*, as she referred to them while struggling with the English Language. Based on the very challenging living conditions and poverty that she encountered in the mining village, one might understand why she felt compelled to take such drastic measures during those very difficult years.

From 1915 to 1940, the family endured, grew, and evolved, often with the help of kind neighbors. For example, a thoughtful mailman kept an eye open for discarded clothing and would distribute it among the homeowners, including Nonno and Nonna. As with all mining families of the time, Nonna and her daughters did their best to stitch clothing from whatever cloth was available, including sacks that previously were filled with bread-baking flour. Mother said flour sacks were also put to such use in her own home when she was a child in Dupont. On one occasion, when Mother's older sister bought a nylon dress slip at a store, Grandfather Nicholo complained sarcastically in broken English, "**Holly Wuud???**" He regarded such clothing as extravagant and should be purchased only by Hollywood movie starlets.

During the Great Depression, the demand for anthracite coal and miners was very weak. To make matters worse, Nonno's outspoken defense of the Mineworkers Union further weakened his opportunity on the few days that mine superintendents selected from the pool of miners standing patiently near the road entrance to the mine. In this critical time of need, the family had to rely on every possible means of placing food on the table. Some of the younger children began going to elementary school; but before walking three miles from Old Boston to the school in Sebastapool (Center of Figure 1), it was mandatory that they work to cultivate and maintain the vegetable gardens that were planted on three sides of the home. Hunger was relatively uncommon, provided everyone worked hard to gather food. In the summer, Nonna often led her children into the hills east of Old Boston to pick buckets of blueberries. The berries were not used to make pies, but were bottled and placed later on fresh (or stale) bread for the morning's breakfast.

Wild dandelions were picked wherever they grew and served as dinner salad. In the fall, wild mushrooms also became available from the nearby forest.

It is very doubtful there were large flocks of robins or sparrows around Old Boston in those years. Dad and his good friend, Sam, once recounted for me how their fathers would shoot and roast these on an open fire for the evening dinner. An amusing anecdote in the region at that time stated that the greatest threat to the bird population were Italian coal miners. Dad and Sam also reminisced about the way they would snare rabbits and woodchucks. For rabbits, a bare steel wire would be formed in the shape of a neck noose and tied to a small tree or large rock adjacent to a rabbit hole. The noose would be placed at just the right circumference and elevation over the exit from the rabbit hole. Woodchuck snares were less humane. Large fishhooks would be attached to a stick and rammed repeatedly into the woodchuck's lair. After some prodding, the angry critter would snap at the probe, which led to its downfall. The animal steadfastly wedged its four legs to the walls of the tunnel and could not be dislodged until becoming weakened under the sustained pressure from the boys, who often took their turn restraining the fishhook, when the other boy became fatigued.

When not in the mine, Nonno did his best to bring wild game and fresh meat to the table. There were also two private reservoirs operated by a major water utility within two or three miles southeast of Old Boston. These were referred to as "The Small Dam" (Gardner Creek Reservoir) and "The Big Dam" (Mill Creek Reservoir). When Nonno could "borrow" a stick or two of dynamite from the mine, the reservoirs would yield a few pounds of perch and sunfish. When I visited an old friend by the name of Tony Ciliberto in Old Boston in 2018, he told me that he remembered Nonno often gave a shotgun with a single shell to his sons and sternly warned them, "*There won't be any dinner for you tonight if you don't bring something home to eat!"* It explained to me how Dad and his brothers eventually became outstanding hunters and riflemen. My old friend, Tony, also said that he and his childhood friends typically darted to the opposite side of the road whenever they walked Old Boston's single roadway past Nonno's house. He didn't clearly explain the reason for the 'cross-over'; but it is a well-known fact that Nonno's dog, "Sport", was the most vicious 'pet' in town. Perhaps the "reason" for the cross-over had more to do with Sport's vicious bark, instead of Nonno's; but Tony's testimony didn't fully support my assumption.

The shack that Nonna inherited from her first husband was truly dilapidated. Nonna and Nonno did their best to seal out the frigid winter weather common to Northeastern Pennsylvania. It is a bit of a mystery to understand how they could have afforded insurance, even for a shanty like that one. Perhaps with a loan from Nonna's sister, Adele in Plains, or from her brother Pacifico Stella in Corklain(Center of Figure 1), they were able to purchase home insurance. One day, while Nonno was at the mine, Dad, who was just a young boy at the time, began running toward the home and yelling, "*MOMMA, THE HOUSE IS ON FIRE!*" Dad recounted that Nonna was standing not far from the shack and sternly responded, "*SHUD UP AND GO PLAY!*" The new home built with the help of the insurance company after the "cooking accident" was a modest two-story wood-framed house built adjacent to the remains of the previous shack. Nonna used the remaining foundation of the previous burned-out shack as an oven for baking home-made bread. Remarkably, when I 'Google Earth' for "*Old Boston Road, Pittston, Pennsylvania*", the map marker sets at the exact location of Nonna's former home near the eastern end of Old Boston Road! After a number of renovations by subsequent owners, it still stands there today.

Sometime around 1934 or 1935, Uncle Ted began working for a kind gentleman who owned an auto sales and repair shop on South Main Street, Pittston. The gentleman's name was Mike Barber, who many years later moved his business, Barber Motors, across the Susquehanna River to Exeter (upper left corner of Figure 1). During such hard times, Uncle Ted's pay was as little as $2 or $3 per day; however, he eventually rose to a supervisory position in the company. With Uncle Ted's assistance, Nonno also persuaded Mr. Barber to let his sons—Uncle Army, Uncle Nello, and Dad—work at the garage after each graduated (1935–1938) from Jenkins Township High School in Sebastapool. In a large photo taken of his 1936 high school graduation class, Dad appears standing in the top row on the school's front steps with one hand on hip, and chin slightly raised. By the proud pose and stern expression on his face, and knowing how he labored in the years that followed, I am quite certain I know precisely what was going through his mind at the moment the photo was snapped. Although no one smiled much in photos taken during that period, his particularly determined pose and expression emphatically says, *"I WILL WORK HARD AND MAKE MONEY!"* Typically, the boys agreed to work at Barber Motors for five or six months without pay until they learned to repair, straighten, or paint cars, or overhaul engines; then they could begin receiving a weekly pay of a few dollars. Even though hardship continued, Nonno's family seemed to enter a new era of improved economic means and life style by 1938. On Saturday evening, even a dime might now be available to view the weekly movie projected on a small screen on the second floor of the Old Boston Italian-American Citizen's Club.

Dad and Mother met at a dance at the Fire Hose House on Main Street, Dupont (Upper right side of Figure 1) in 1939, across from 323 Main Street where Mother lived with her parents, three sisters, and four brothers. The music of Tommy Dorsey and Glen Miller is nostalgic for me today, even though its era of prominence existed before I was old enough to remember it. Nevertheless, I can clearly picture my Father and Mother dancing to that very classic, lively music. Before their marriage, Mother wrote in her diary that when returning to Dupont on a bus from Pittston one day, one boyfriend was standing at the first bus stop on Main Street, while Dad was a little further east at the second stop. Both were awaiting Mother's arrival. She wrote that at the spur of the moment, she decided to tell the driver that she was getting off at the second stop. I joked (poorly) with her many years later, "*Whew, that was a close call. I almost didn't make it! If I knew the bus driver's name, I would certainly give him a bottle of Schenley every Christmas.*" Dad and Mother married in 1940 and moved in with Nonna and Nonno at the old homestead on the east side of Old Boston. One or two years later, they rented an apartment in a small house on the west side of Old Boston where I was born, and where we lived for two years. In a re-visit to Old Boston in 2019 with my Mother, I confirmed that the small house still stands today on the east side of Old Boston Road. I observed it as a sagging, vacant, deteriorated structure of which I concluded and joked to Mother, "*It's probably in the same condition I created and left it seventy-six years ago!*" To my surprise, however, Mother somberly responded that my assumption had merit.

CHAPTER IV

FOCUS AND INTENSITY (1940–1950)

I was born in 1942, and in later years I rhetorically asked my family and friends, "*Now tell me, if my family reports that Nonno was terrible and mean, then **why was I named after him??**"* In response to my own question I said, "*Well then, there's only one possible explanation: Everyone must have looked down in the crib and concluded: "**What an awful, terrible baby! We should name him after his Grandfather!**"* Based on this sarcastic reasoning, I concluded that over time, Nonno's bad reputation has been exaggerated and is very likely undeserved and unfair. My response to my own question to my family was my humorously sarcastic way of communicating my belief that Nonno's pranks, though severe, were miss-judged. After all, Nonna's youngest off-spring, Aunt Ada, always said I was a cute, very chunky little baby, and not 'terrible and mean'. Throughout the seventy years of our wonderful friendship, Aunt Ada Rostock would grin broadly whenever she saw me and always welcome me with, "*Hello, Roundy-Ball?*"

The following story further reinforces my conclusion concerning Nonno's inaccurate and undeserved reputation for extreme meanness. According to Uncle Gildo, one miner at the Old Boston Club House bragged to Nonno about the money the miner's son made weekly at the coal colliery. Referring to him by Nonno's nickname, the miner sarcastically asked Nonno, "*SCA-TAY*, *how much do your boys make in the auto shop, SCA-TAY*?" The miner knew Dad and his brothers made nothing as they worked hard to learn a trade during the depression. Nonno replied, "*I don't care how much money your son makes at the colliery. I don't want my boys in the mines!*" Now, if Nonno was as mean as his reputation suggested, wouldn't he insist his sons work in the mines, and also share their paycheck with Nonno to pay for their living expenses?? I also was told that after Uncle Army, Dad, and Uncle Nello graduated from high school (1935-38), Nonno approached Mike Barber at Barber Motors and suggested, "*I'll buy a car from you if you give my boys a job in your repair shop.*" Uncle Gildo's stories affirm my contention that Nonno's 'crude humor' and severe pranks were overstated as "Mean", by Family and friends. Not only did Nonno decline to have his sons bring him a paycheck by laboring at the mine, but he also shelled out his own money to help them get training for a job that initially didn't pay anything in return! Hence, I rest my case: Nonno **was** a good man.

Nevertheless, Dad became an anthracite miner in 1942, one year after Nonno passed away. One evening, Dad returned home from the auto shop and found his younger brother picking at a small coal outcrop about 250 feet east of the family home in Old Boston. Uncle Gildo found the seam and was taking the coal to Nonna's house stove, and the bread-baking oven in the yard outside the house. In the days that followed, Dad continued to hand-dig the small outcrop each evening after work at the auto shop, until he decided to quit his job at the auto shop and devote all of his effort to the new dog-hole. With the same creativity and energy he displayed throughout his life, Dad either purchased or rented an old Ford Model A or Model T, removed the rear wheels, and rigged the axle with a cable drum to pull a small coal car out of the mine. He built a wood chute at the mouth of the mine so that the coal car could be emptied into a dump-truck. He hand-dug a sloping ramp so that the truck could be backed down under the chute. A friend from Old Boston, Gino Popple, had a small dump-truck and became Dad's partner in the new dog-hole. It is unknown if they mined the coal legally by paying a royalty to the large coal company that owned the mining rights, or if they mined the coal without the knowledge of the coal company. Such small dog-holes, operated without the knowledge of the coal's rightful owners, were referred to as "boot-legging". I suspect that soon, the owner found out and demanded royalty or lease payments. Such payment was usually around 10 percent of the value of the sale at the "Breaker" where the coal was delivered by dump-truck. There, the coal was crushed, screened, washed, and sorted for retail sales to homes and industry. My sketch of an anthracite breaker similar to the one-hundred, more or less, that once dotted Northeastern Pennsylvania, is shown in Figure 2.

Mother recalls that even as a tot only three or four years old, I took substantial interest in the Popple and Scatena Coal Company. When Dad descended the cellar stairs each evening to remove his dirty mining clothes and clean up, Mother recalls that I would call out down the stairs, "*Pete, how many cars of coal today? Pete, how many loads did Gino make with the truck?*" Of course, I can't recall the exact questions or Dad's response; but the quantity probably didn't earn Dad and Gino more than a few dollars each after they purchased supplies and paid the two or three men on their payroll. After all, they had no motor driven loaders, and all coal had to be hand-shoveled into the coal car. Dad also once recounted how he would enter the mine around 5:00 each morning and make many trips in and out of the tunnel, carrying two buckets to remove accumulated groundwater so that miners arriving at 7:00 a.m. would be able to work in a reasonably dry mine chamber.

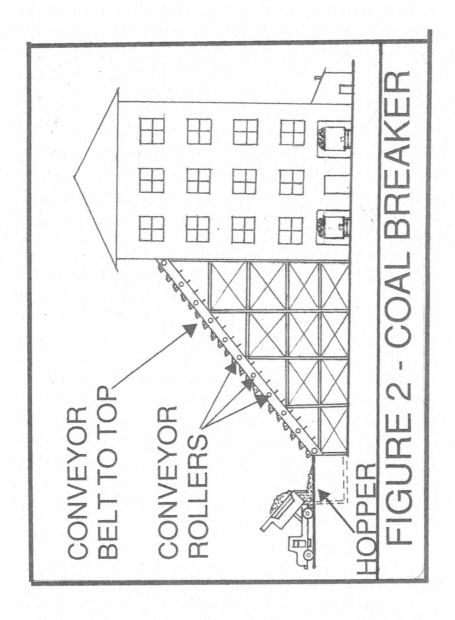

CONVEYOR BELT TO TOP

CONVEYOR ROLLERS

HOPPER

FIGURE 2 - COAL BREAKER

Nevertheless, it wouldn't be long before Dad could replace the makeshift "Ford Hoist" with a real mine hoist and purchase a small water pump. Even after Dad had his first serious mine accident around 1943—a broken leg—he was undeterred. After hobbling on crutches for several weeks, Dad started a new dog-hole about one-quarter mile south of the initial one, in a rocky, wooded area outside Old Boston known as "Pickaway". He and Gino built a wood "tipple", installed a used mine hoist in a shanty, and hoisted the coal cars up a steep slope to the tipple, which could hold forty or fifty tons. (See Figure 3 for a typical coal tipple.) As at many exhausted and abandoned coal mines near Old Boston and in The Wyoming Valley, Pickaway is now covered by a huge industrial storage building.

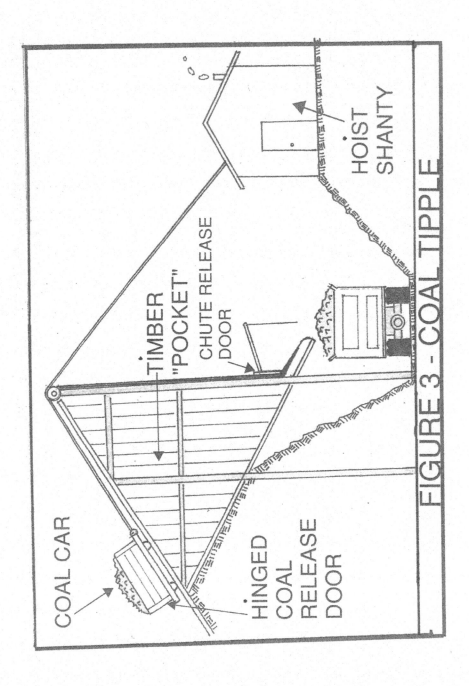

FIGURE 3 - COAL TIPPLE

Around 1947, I began to have occasional opportunities to see the mine. Dad had asked his younger brother, Uncle Elmo, to leave Jenkins Township High School in the tenth grade, and begin hauling the coal to the breaker with the small dump-truck that Dad and Gino owned. Dad later expressed regret at taking his kid brother out of school; but I am certain that he did so to improve the economic welfare of his mother, brother, and sister who still lived in Old Boston. By this time, Dad and Mother had moved out of Old Boston and rented an apartment on Ziegler Street in Dupont, around the corner from where Mother's parents lived on 323 Main Street near the Dupont Hose House. I can't recall my childhood toys; but I can easily recall my excitement whenever Uncle Elmo would pick me up at our apartment in Dupont. He would take me with him to load the truck at the tipple and haul the coal to the breaker. As shown in the picture for a coal breaker in Figure 2, a slow moving conveyor dragged the coal up to the top of the breaker from the hopper at the bottom where Uncle Elmo dumped the coal. After countless trips to the breaker during my early childhood, and to this day, I can recall the soft, repetitious sound of the squeaking steel rollers as they rotated very slowly under the conveyor belt that carried the coal to the top of the breaker. It is utterly amazing to me how the opening scenes at a coal breaker in "The Molly Maguires" Hollywood movie, utilizes soft music with Irish harp and piccolo that so accurately interprets the subtle, three-note rhythm that I distinctly remember emanating from the steel rollers under the breaker's conveyor, sixty to seventy years ago. I am willing to bet that particular mechanical sound was the reference that Henry Mancini used as an inspiration to interpret and transform the actual environment of an anthracite breaker into his beautiful music for that film. It seems most likely the iconic music composer visited other operating breakers in the area to gain a realistic sense for the environment, prior to writing the music fifty years ago.

In 1947, Dad and Gino bought a big, green Brockway dump-truck similar to the one shown in Figure 4. At age seventeen or eighteen, Uncle Elmo artistically painted the underside frame, wheel hubs, and front grille a glistening, bright yellow. He also built up the truck's steel box with wood sideboards so it could carry a maximum load, and he blasted the air horn at every slow driver in front of him. I remember the brightly colored green and yellow dump-truck as a polished 'work of art'. With the built-up sideboards, the heavy Brockway with a load of coal was usually over the State legal gross weight limit for a single-axle, Z-license truck. The legal limit dictated that he not load the truck with more than approximately eleven tons of coal. Nevertheless, Uncle Elmo always heaped the truck as much as possible. State police patrolled the highways with portable scales; however, my Uncle did not seem to care and was constantly ticketed for over-loading. The penalty was usually a cash fine or a night in the jail in Dupont. To the best of my knowledge, Uncle Elmo never paid any fines for truck over-load.

Between the ages of five and eight, I often asked my parents to allow me to spend some evenings with my Uncle Elmo, Aunt Ada, and Nonna in Old Boston so I could enjoy the excitement of riding in the roaring green and yellow monster between the mine and breaker the next day. During dinner one evening, Nonna intentionally gave me too much homemade wine and I cried with dizziness. I can still recall, even after more than 70 years, the mischievous, wide grin on her face as she backed out of the bedroom, where she had led me to sleep off her prank. Eventually, I concluded that this was just one example of where Dad got the inspiration for his 'troublesome' sense of humor from both Nonno and Nonna; but more about 'intense pranks' in an upcoming chapter.

CHUNK "DRESSING"

CANOPY

AIR HORN

TAIL GATE

WOOD SIDEBOARDS

BROCKWAY

FIGURE 4 – 1947 BROCKWAY DUMPTRUCK

One day, the Brockway was stopped near the top of a steep, snowy hill on the dirt road leading to the mine, and I got out of the truck to watch my Uncle shovel ashes in front of the rear tires. Suddenly, while we were standing in front of the truck almost at the top of the hill, the hand brake inexplicably disengaged and the truck sped down the steep hill backward. Uncle Elmo ran like a deer to catch up to it, jumped behind the wheel as the truck ran away faster and faster, and steered it by viewing behind the truck through his rear view mirror as it zoomed backward. At a very high speed, he maneuvered the truck backward around a sharp ninety degree curve at the bottom of the hill, barely missing the edge of a deep ravine on one side of the sharp curve. This was just one of many "near misses" that I witnessed in Anthracite Boot Camp. However, I always marveled at my Uncle's athletic ability. As a young boy, I thoroughly enjoyed riding in the dump-truck and was impressed by his somewhat aggressive driving skills. I also concluded that much of his aggression was designed to entertain me. I strongly suspect that my Uncle would occasionally steer the truck along the edge of deep strip mine pits merely to give me a 'thrill'. I have since con- cluded that not only was he a natural 'dare-devil', but he also enjoyed showing me a good time. At one such pit, fully loaded with coal, the truck had to make a sharp 90-degree turn to the left, again, barely skirting a deep strip mine on the right side at about five or ten miles an hour. There was also a large pothole on the right side of the rocky road so that the fully loaded, top-heavy truck tipped precariously even further to my right as we rounded the curve. I looked down through the window on my right side at the twenty-five or thirty foot deep pit two or three feet away, and quickly glanced a startled look back toward my Uncle behind the steering wheel. I can recall that by the expression on his face, even he suddenly felt uncomfortable with his planned, or unplanned, "thrill", as the top-heavy truck slowly tilted toward the pit. Fortunately, the truck gradually leveled off as it rolled up and out of the depression, and around the curve. When we returned later for the next load of coal, Dad obviously wasn't thrilled, either, by what he had seen. Dad had already placed large slabs of rock in the pothole to force Uncle Elmo to steer the truck further from the edge of the deep pit on subsequent loads.

When visiting with my Uncle to enjoy the excitement of the big green Brockway, however, my biggest challenge was not in avoiding Nonna's vino, or enduring his fabricated 'dump-truck thrills'. He hadn't met Aunt Jean yet, and my greatest challenge was to ignore the semi-nude photos of Marilyn Monroe on calendar pages that he had taped overhead across the ceiling of the truck's cab. Apparently, Marilyn had become quite famous in posing for such calendars prior to her Hollywood stardom. I also suspected that despite the number of calendar photos, my Uncle probably wasn't interested in the calendar's dates or true purpose. Also difficult to ignore was the colorful rendering of a little puppy pulling at the hem of a leggy model's partially buttoned negligee as she reached down through her doorway to pick up a newspaper on her front porch. I'm sure it was the little puppy that made my recollection unforgettable. Riding in my Uncle's big shiny, green Brockway also helped develop my appreciation for fine art. I'm certain it was the "art" that also impressed me. While touring the Sistine Chapel at the Vatican in Rome forty years later, I joked (not so poorly) to a puzzled tour guide that Michelangelo's classical art on the chapel ceiling, *reminds me of my Uncle Elmo's dump-truck*".

I also began to meet Dad's partner, Gino Popple, frequently, and I came to admire the soft-spoken, husky brute greatly. When I was a boy, he seemed hard and unapproachable. However, one day when I was only six or seven years old, I was riding in his pick-up with him when he stopped at a gas station and handed me an ice cream treat when he returned to the pickup. I politely exclaimed, *"Wow, thank you!"* Without turning his head, which seemed unsupported by a neck, and out of the slits in the right corner of his eye, he sarcastically grinned and softly muttered out of the side of his mouth above a chiseled chin, *"Cut the crap, kid!"* As time passed, I gradually realized it was all part of his "John Wayne Tough Guy Act", and he was hiding a generous heart of gold.

When I was between the ages of five and eight, Dad began taking me along to the mine more and more. Dad's version of 'take-your-child-to-work day' occurred every week or two, and I suspect it was mostly for my own amusement. It's also possible he sensed that I was intensely interested. One morning at about 1:00 a.m., he and Uncle Elmo attached a cable to a large wood shanty that was mounted to the top of wood skids at an abandoned mine in Laflin (Bottom of Figure 1). I then watched my Uncle tow the shanty behind the Brockway, skidding it along the surface of Highway 315 to Old Boston. A little old retired miner by the name of Deiniso Tucci (pronounced Too-chee) subsequently rented the shanty from Nonna, and also paid her for cooked meals and homemade red wine. Nonna also catered homemade dinners and wine from time to time for other immigrant miners who lived alone in nearby, tiny shanties. During the Great Depression in Old Boston, Nonna's basement had been a popular (but illegal) "Speak-easy" for miners in the settlement. One such miner was known as "Jack the Spaniard". For some odd reason, strange nicknames seemed to be common in Old Boston. Some I can recall in the small, iso-lated community of about two hundred homes were: "Floppy", "Jiggs", "Schnail-er", "Frosty", "Chick-a-dee", "Run-dee", "Beaver", and others. More than likely, the nicknames were indicative of the very friendly social environment common within a small, tight-knit mining village.

Tucci often spoke with pride of his World War I service under U.S Army General "Black Jack" Pershing; but Tucci turned comic whenever Nonna requested payment after a few glasses of vino. With a toothless smile and face flushed red as the wine he drank, the friendly little man typically yelled out his comical response to Nonna's request for payment: ***"TRY GET!"*** It was also entertaining to watch the two drinking home-made wine on Nonna's back porch, snacking her raw, garden-grown garlic, and arguing intensely about the destination of each overhead plane that they observed departing from the Scranton-Wilkes Barre airport in Avoca (Upper right corner of Figure 1). I sometimes wondered how many immigrant miners ended up like Tucci, after being 'led' to America and a path of extreme hardship by exaggerated ads for miners circulated in Europe. Initially, there was the WOP (Without Official Papers) tag on his lapel that also noted his destination. The tag enabled the agent at Ellis Island to lead Tucci to the proper entry desk, bus, or train. Then, Tucci was led into a dangerous mine where he would battle to survive and make one or two dollars each day. Later, his adopted country would grant him citizenship only after he was led to World War I in Europe, where he continued to battle to survive. Subsequently, he was led back into dangerous anthracite mines and, later, battled to breathe through blackened lungs lacerated by coal dust. Throughout my life, I have never observed greater suffering than that which an ex-miner endures when stricken with Anthrasilicosis; i.e. "Black Lung" disease. Finally, and at a relatively early age, Tucci's decimated body would be transported from his tiny wood shanty near our home, and carried by a few friends to a soon overgrown grave in the small town cemetery, where he is soon forgotten. I suspect there were thousands of other "Tuccis" who were "led" down similar sad paths after immigration to the anthracite coal fields.

Other than occasionally running to fetch a shovel or tool for Dad, I certainly could not contribute much labor, and never entered the mines in those very early years before 1950. On countless occasions, I would be left in the pickup while he crawled into some old abandoned, partially collapsed mine while prospecting for coal. Dad did not have any political affiliations to give him mining opportunities. He crawled through black, underground caverns alone and relentlessly to find anthracite. I sometimes sat for hours alone in the pickup, hopeful that he would re-emerge soon and safely. When I was eight years old, it became apparent Dad wanted me to learn to work. In 1950, he decided to build the Midway Restaurant, with our new home on the second floor. The restaurant and home were on the east side of State Highway 315, one mile south of Dupont. He would work in the mine during the day and on the construction of the restaurant and home in the evening. He set up a portable, electric concrete mixer in the new basement and loaded it with cement, sand, stone, and water. At age eight, there wasn't much I could do to assist with loading the tall concrete mixer; but once he tilted the revolving mixer drum and deposited the concrete on the ground, he needed me to guide one end of the screed board that he and I moved along the top of the fresh concrete to level it. Today, proud construction contractors with thirty-plus years of experience turn dis-believing when I tell them my first construction experience occurred seventy years ago.

Although he had hired a carpenter, Cielio Migliosi, to help build the new home and restaurant during the day, Dad cut and nailed wood studs, joists, and plywood flooring each evening. I helped a little by holding the lumber as he cut and nailed it. On one occasion, he had a spotlight positioned so we could work on the roof into the evening. Uncle Mike Vigilante visited the construction site with a carload of his little nieces and nephews and was taking them to an outdoor movie

– The Comerford Drive-In Theater - that had just been built around 1949, across the highway from our new restaurant and home. He lowered his car window and asked Dad if I could join him, my sister, and my cousins in their visit to the outdoor theater. Dad hesitated, and then politely said, *"No, I need him."* I don't recall feeling even the slightest disappointment at the time. In fact, I quite likely took personal pride in Dad's announcement of my 'manly importance' in the presence of my (still) pretty sister, Carol, and my friendly, close, smaller cousins.

During the following Christmas or the next, I told Mother that I would like to give Dad a black lunch bucket, including coffee thermos, as a gift to be placed under the Christmas tree. I had noticed that almost all miners carried their lunch and coffee thermos in similar hinged, black metal lunch pails; but Dad carried his sandwiches in only a brown paper bag. I felt terrific while Dad opened his gift; but he probably felt the bucket shaped like a black mail box with leather handle was "too conventional". Besides, he rarely took the time to eat lunch, anyway, while loading coal. I saw him later that evening take a steel nail and quietly inscribe my own name in the white enamel coating on the inside of the lunch bucket. Initially, I was puzzled by his action. Soon, however, I began to understand the meaning of the 'writing on the wall' of the lunch bucket, and Dad's plan for my upcoming "enlistment" in Anthracite Boot Camp.

CHAPTER V

FIRST DAY OF ANTHRACITE BOOT CAMP (1951)

I had many close friends in grade school and on my Little League baseball team; however, beginning when I was nine years old, anthracite dog-holes and small wood shanties became my primary 'playground'. By this point in time, Dad had decided that the quickest way to start a dog-hole was to uncover the vein of coal with the bulldozer, dig a pit that could store eighty to hundred tons of coal near the entrance to the mine, and have Uncle Elmo load the coal on the Brockway with a steam-shovel. My sketch of a steam-shovel similar to Dad's is shown in Figure 5. The machine had a diesel engine; but the name was a hold-over from the old days when such equipment was steam-driven. Just as Uncle Elmo built up the box of the Brockway with wood planks to haul a maximum load, Dad welded steel plates to enlarge the three-quarter ton bucket of the steam-shovel so it could lift more than one ton of coal. Maximum speed and production were essential in every phase of their work. Uncle Mike Vigilante often coached me to play baseball with what he called "Jinnegar". The web defines it as a now outdated term baseball players in the Eastern U.S. used prior to World War II to describe how the game should be played with energy, focus, and intensity. Dad, Gino, and Uncle Elmo mined and loaded anthracite with tons of Jinnegar. Even when I see a dump-truck without side boards today, I intuitively conclude, *"There goes a guy without Jinnegar!"* Why haul only 8 or 9 tons of payload when you can haul 11 or 12 tons within legal limits? Believe it or not, I even see dump-trucks on construction projects today with a 10 ton capacity; but carrying only 5 or 6 tons! I figure they must be paid by the hour, instead of on the basis of real production.

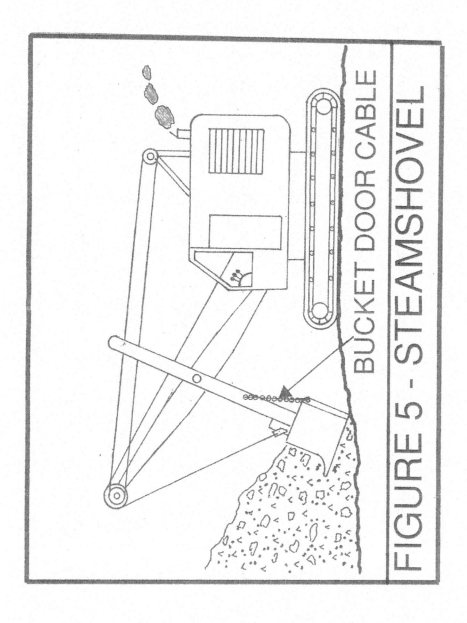

FIGURE 5 - STEAMSHOVEL

BUCKET DOOR CABLE

From inside the shanty, I (very skillfully, of course) operated a lever-controlled mechanical loader (Figure 6) that pulled a bucket or scoop (Figure 7) with a coal capacity of about one ton. Again, with outstanding creativity and focused ambition, Dad had a welder fabricate the bucket so that it was lightweight and could be lifted by a single miner, and strategically placed behind a pile of coal deep inside the mine. The frame of the bucket was fabricated with lightweight hollow tubing instead of solid, heavy steel bars. The bottom of the vertical side plates were curved inward so that it could slice its way deeply into the pile to scoop up the coal. Similar equipment exists at the Anthracite Museum in Scranton; but in comparison, the museum equipment is heavy, awkward, and certainly not as efficient. The mechanical loader was about the size of a large kitchen table. One section contained a 30 horsepower electric motor if electricity existed at the mine, or a 30 horsepower gasoline engine if no electricity existed. The second section contained two cable-coiling drums, each operated by depressing a steel lever at the top of each drum. The 'main' and 'tail' rope cables can be seen in Figures 6 and 7. When the left lever was depressed, the left drum reeled in the main three-quarter inch diameter steel cable that dragged the loaded coal scoop out of the mine. By pressing down harder on the lever, the cable drum rotated more rapidly and the scoop traveled faster. When the right lever was depressed, the right drum reeled in a one-half inch diameter steel tail rope cable. The tail rope ran from the drum back into the mine, around a steel pulley at the mine face where the men were working, and returned out to the back end of the scoop. The tail rope through the pulley dragged the scoop back to the miners after the coal in the scoop was piled in the pit near the steam-shovel. A dog-hole might function for six to twelve months because the mechanical loader only had a horizontal mining range of 700 or 800 feet. Then, the equipment was moved several hundred feet to a new dog-hole in the same vein, or Dad might discover a more profitable vein elsewhere within a few miles of Pittston.

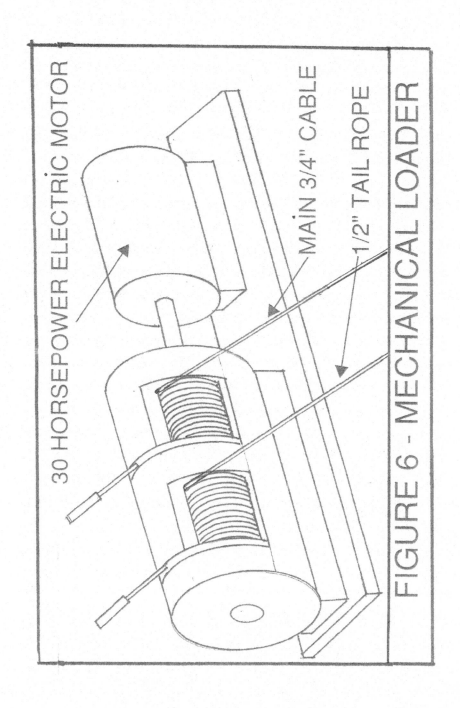

FIGURE 6 – MECHANICAL LOADER

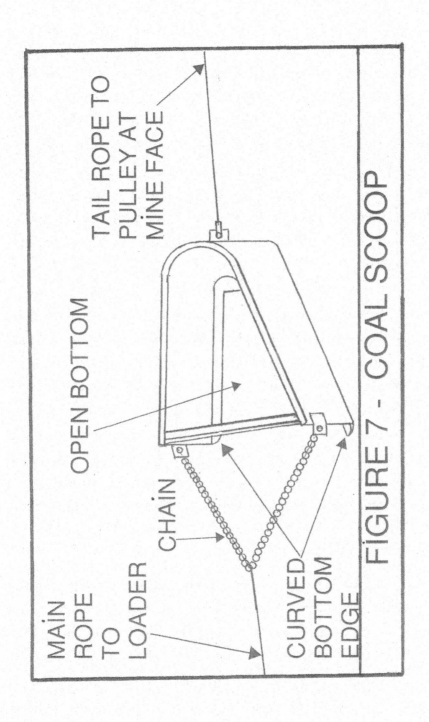

TAIL ROPE TO PULLEY AT MINE FACE

OPEN BOTTOM

CHAIN

MAIN ROPE TO LOADER

CURVED BOTTOM EDGE

FIGURE 7 – COAL SCOOP

From the winter of 1951 to the summer of 1959, I usually was behind the mechanical loader at Dad's various dog-holes when I was not in elementary or high school. My first day of Anthracite Boot Camp training occurred during my Christmas vacation in the fifth grade. I rode with Dad to his dog-hole on Irish Hill, (Right side of Figure 1) about one mile east of Old Boston. We accessed the mine by driving the two-lane paved road east from Dupont through Suscon (right side of Fig. 1) and then traveled about two miles south on a dirt road owned and operated by the DuPont de Nemours dynamite powder company. Irish Hill is now totally covered by huge industrial warehouses and tractor-trailer terminals. The powder company moved out after coal mining and the need for dynamite, gradually diminished. However, in 1951, the powder company made and stored dynamite in several small steel buildings on Irish Hill. The powder company allowed Dad to use the very private road because he agreed to help them grade and maintain the road with his bulldozer. The winter weather was bitter and the mechanical loader was in a 15' × 15' × 8' high wood shanty that had a small coal stove in one corner. Heavy winds often prevailed from the west, crossed the Wyoming Valley, and wracked the hillside and shanty. Today, eleven or twelve huge electrical generating wind turbines now line the top of nearby Bald Mountain, just slightly east of, and above Irish Hill where the mine was located. The wind turbines and their giant propeller blades dominate the eastern skyline when viewed from The Wyoming Valley, down below.

Dad explained to me that when he touched two wires together three times inside the mine, the bell in the shanty would ring three times, and it meant I had to depress the lever on the tail rope drum to pull the bucket back into the mine. He started to say, "*And when you hear one bell—*", at which time I interrupted him and said, "*I know. It means I stop the bucket.*" Dad and his friend, Sam, laughed and Sam said, *"He already knows!"* Of course, I had watched other operators, and the signaling system was, in fact, very simple. From a stopped position, a single bell meant to pull the bucket (scoop) forward very slowly because a miner was kneeling on top of the scoop, and using his weight to press the scoop into the side of the coal pile. Two bells meant the miner was off the scoop, the scoop was full, and it should be pulled out to the storage pit at full speed. Twenty bells meant the miners wanted me to stack six or seven mine props in front of the scoop outside the mine entrance, coil the main cable around the group of wood props, and drag the scoop and props back to the miners with the loader. Then, the miners would measure, cut, and prop the roof where the previous cut of sixty to eighty tons of coal had been drilled, blasted, and removed. The wood props were cut from the forest and supplied by a local timber company. Ten slow rings from the bell was the signal that I should disconnect the wire from the bell and reconnect it to an electric switchbox in the shanty. After I turned the switch on, the miners could use an electric drill to horizontally auger holes into the hard anthracite to insert sticks of dynamite to blast the next cut of coal.

After my initial shanty/classroom training, Dad and Sam entered the dog-hole, and I could hear them as they shuffled back into the mine. Dad was probably assuring Sam that I knew what to do, and they would be safe riding atop the scoop. Suddenly, I heard a frightening, ground-shaking **"THUD!"** coming from inside the mine. Then I heard Dad and Sam running back out toward the mine entrance. They came out and were visibly relieved to see that I was standing calmly at the shanty door, and had not tossed gasoline from a nearby container onto the dormant stove fire. The 'thud' that the three of us heard was a roof collapse in an abandoned mine chamber that interconnected nearby with our dog-hole. The experience with the cave-in on my very first day of Anthracite Boot Camp was both ominous and unforgettable.

My biggest fear as a nine-year-old at that mine during winter months was not the heavy west-to-east winds blasting Irish Hill, nor the sub-freezing temperatures, nor operating the mechanical coal loader, nor manipulation of electrical switchboxes. By far, my biggest fear was: **HUNGRY BLACK BEARS!** We were in a remote wooded area, two miles from the nearest homes, and I had heard many stories about bear-hunting in that region. There was a large axe in the shanty, and I always made sure the axe was within arm's reach while I was operating the loader. One day, I was entirely certain I saw a bear track in the snow just behind the shanty, and I refused to respond to the bell signals from the miners. Dad came out and asked, "*What's wrong?*" In terror, I pointed and shuttered, "**THERE'S A BEAR TRACK!**" He laughed and said it was just the sunlight reflecting off the glass windowpane and melting the snow in spots. Nevertheless, I always kept the axe near my side, and in the summer, the axe also lessened my fear of rattlers and copperhead snakes that I had heard slither among the nearby rock ledges. Over time, the miners caught on to the purpose of the axe that was always at my side, and they never let me forget my fear of bears. In fact, they made every effort to cultivate my fear with an occasional prank.

About 600 feet from this mine, there was a large pipeline that the local water company used to augment the storage at the reservoir behind the Small Dam. One day during the summer, the miners asked me to go to the pipeline and fill a few water bottles in a valve opening at the top of the pipe. While filling the bottles, the brush behind me began to rustle violently, and from within the brush came a distinct, loud **"GROWL"**! I immediately took off running in the opposite direction and down the dirt road nearby that was the access to the mine, flinging the water bottles aside along the way. As I ran toward the miners, Dad asked (again), "*What's wrong?*" Terrified, I yelled, "**THERE'S**

A BEAR CHASING ME!" The miners laughed, and I learned that Sam had sent another miner to "growl" the role of the bear. Many years later, whenever I would visit Sam Casciani and his wife at their home in Browntown, Sam would retell the story to Hilda with certain embellishments. He suggested that I even lost my shoes while running frantically from the bear that I thought was chasing me. It seems that throughout my youthful mining career, I was the subject of miners' pranks, and perhaps that contributed to the development of my own (advanced) skills in similar experiences with friends; but more about "anthracite pranks" in an upcoming chapter.

Dad never lost his family's 'depression era need' to hunt and put fresh meat on the dinner table, and it did not matter whether the hunt was within the State's legal hunting season. He usually carried a vintage 12-gage Fox double-barrel shotgun behind the seat of the pickup and would quickly jamb the brakes whenever any unlucky critter crossed in front of us on the dirt road leading to the mine. On one occasion, his target was a flock of someone's home-bred pigeons. I recall one of the wounded birds diving beak first, smashing kamikaze style into the side of the pickup, right next to where I was standing, and forcing me to jump aside. I obviously picked up on the habit of "nabbing critters", and one day while riding with another miner, I asked him to stop when a woodchuck crossed the dirt road. I stoned the animal and placed his carcass in our basement until such time that I could skin him and clean the meat. An hour later, I heard Mother's loud shriek as the shadow of the large varmint scampered around in the darkness of our basement! On more than one occasion, Mother was not happy about the varmints that I brought home for dinner. Besides, the Great Depression had faded away twelve to fifteen years earlier.

Occasionally after work, and before I was old enough to carry a hunting rifle, Dad and I would walk into the hills near the mine on

Irish Hill in search of deer. He would wave his arms and point in the direction he wanted me to circle through the woods to flush out any deer to the point where he would be posted with his double-barrel. For example, he might say, "*Walk down this trail for 5 minutes, or about 1,000 feet, until you come to another trail off to the left. Take that for about 5 minutes, then turn left and come back up the hill through the woods, and I will be standing on that rock ledge(as he pointed) over there.*" Of course, I couldn't admit to him I was confused; but I wandered in the general direction he pointed, and eventually turned back up the hill through the thick woods and swamps. One day, however, I heard the old Fox shotgun ring out, Dad came over to where he spotted me walking, and told me to follow him up the hill to the kill. He steadied the deer's carcass on his left shoulder with his left arm and carried the Fox shotgun in his right hand, as I walked along behind him down to the pickup. Most boys thought their Dad was superman, but I didn't **think** so. I **knew** Dad was Superman and no one could tell me different! I also recall feeling quite content with my part in the team effort. About three or four years later, after I became old enough for a hunting license, my teamwork during a similar 'deer flush' did not go so well. After Dad provided directions, I wandered, again confused, through an opening in a fence line in Suscon. I soon found myself standing in the center of a complex of dynamite storage buildings with my new 16-gage shotgun. Workers yelled frantically and angrily as I scurried back through the fence opening. Their nervousness was quite understandable, since one or two of their co-workers from Dupont had been killed in an accidental dynamite explosion at that site only a few months earlier.

Dad's 12 gage double barrel Fox shotgun had an interesting history. Sometime during the Great Depression, a series of well-publicized crimes were committed in Old Boston and the weapon was never recovered before or during the trial of the accused. As a young boy, Dad came across the hiding place in the forest where the accused had stashed the weapon to avoid incrimination. Nonno hunted with the gun for years afterward, and Nonna passed it on to Dad after Nonno died.

Besides deer hunting, Dad had a passion for accordion music, but when he was a boy, buying an accordion and paying for lessons was out of the question during The Great Depression. One evening in 1951, he walked into our home crudely playing a semi-recognizable tune. It was his favorite, "Mona Lisa," on a used accordion he had purchased. He stopped playing and sternly announced to me, "*You're going to start taking lessons and you'll be the best around!*" I was very surprised because we had never discussed accordion lessons previously. Dad was bewildered when I responded tearfully. With a puzzled expression on his face, he turned to Mother who had to explain to him, "*He's afraid of disappointing you.*" It wasn't easy to avoid disappointing Dad. He wanted me to excel at everything. When I was nine, he visited one of my little league games in Dupont just in time to see me strike out in the bottom of the ninth inning to lose the game for my team. On the way home, I shrunk down in the seat as, glaring out of the corner of his eye, he softly admonished, "*You had to strike out?*" There has been a similar situation commercialized on TV recently where the father gently consoles the boy on the way home. Dad would not have been ideal for the father's role in that commercial. Now that I think about it, I also would have failed the screen test for the role of the 'consoling father', many years later after watching my own son's initial Pop Warner football games. For many years my son, Pete, reminds me of the time after one of his games that I admonished him for his lack of jinnegar in firing off the defensive line. After returning to our backyard after one of his games, I told him to get on the ground on all fours. With my left hand gripping the back of his football shoulder pads, and my right hand gripping the back of the waist band on his football trousers, I counted, "**1, 2, 3, HIKE!**" ....and launched him five yards. During his subsequent games, with other fathers standing next to me on the sidelines, I may have appeared disinterested, but somewhat restless. In reality, my hands on hips, folded arms, or hand swipe through my hair, were well-rehearsed signals that told Pete precisely how and where I wanted him to fire off the defensive line. To confirm he was not just looking in my direction only to humor me, I also required that he acknowledge receipt and understanding of each of my signals by glancing in my direction and pretending to adjust his facemask. Parents and coaches were always puzzled when Pete sometimes threw the opposing quarterback to the ground, even before the opposing team's center hiked the ball to the quarterback! Now in the years that followed, my challenge has been to help Pete control his jinnegar.

Two or three years after my ninth-inning strike-out, Dad enjoyed taking other miners to my little league games to watch me play when I was older and more skillful. I also learned to play the accordion decently, mostly because Dad sternly directed me to practice each evening. A few years later at the Cetta Parrish music store on the square in Scranton, my accordion teacher, Arnold Gammaitoni, winced at the sight of my coal encrusted keyboard hands and fingernails. Arnold was originally from the mining village of New Boston, and was a life-long friend of Dad's family in Old Boston. Arnold closed his office door after I stepped out, and from a distance outside the glass wall of his office, I could see Arnold looking up at Dad and taking him to task about my labor at the mine. Dad listened politely and quietly; but my thoughtful accordion teacher soon realized it was like water off a duck's back. Little did Arnold know that like Dad, I was indifferent to the coal crust and work. Looking back today, I feel very strongly and thankful that the years I spent working with Dad not only enriched my life experience, but also inspired me later in life to do my best as a family man, citizen, and professional engineer.

To the best of my knowledge, my performance operating the mechanical loader in my first year was satisfactory, as it would be for the next seven and one-half years. On one or two occasions, Sam told Dad that I did not operate the loader very well when Dad was not in the mine, and that I operated it much better when Dad was there. He was probably right and fortunate that Dad was almost always there. On those rare occasions that he was unhappy with my performance, Sam would give me a blast of very rapid 30+ bell rings to let me know he was perturbed. I think it was mostly his way of teasing me, as he always seemed to enjoy doing, even when we hunted together a few years later. After I shot a deer, Sam would say, *"You should have shot two."* Sam Casciani was best man at Mother and Dad's wedding, a hard-working miner, and my great personal friend, until he passed away in 2011 at age ninety-three.

CHAPTER VI

THE MINE ON IRISH HILL (1952)

The miners from Old Boston had names for all of the hills and valleys east of the settlement - names like Irish Hill, Dunn-ee's, Pinch-koo's, Jumper's, etc. I suspect the names originated from the names of miners or families that lived in a shanty on that forested hill or in that remote valley many years earlier. At the mine on Irish Hill, coal production and Dad's good fortune began to escalate, and Dad decided to start a second mine nearby. Not only was the vein thicker than any Dad mined previously, but it was also flat, well defined, and only overlain by twenty-five to thirty feet of good, solid roof rock. By drilling and blasting the rock and excavating a large pit with the bulldozer, anthracite veins near the surface could be quickly exposed so new dog-holes could be created. Dad and Gino had purchased a brand new Caterpillar D-7 bulldozer, with the help of insurance money, after their little World War II surplus A-C International dozer toppled approximately eighty feet into a deep strip mine after Dad jumped clear. The old dozer had a bad habit of jumping out of gear and that likely led to the accident. I've also often wondered if Dad's training during Nonna's 'shud up and go play' house fire in Chapter III also may have contributed to the 'accident'.

At the new dog-hole on Irish Hill, I helped Dad build a wood ramp up and out of the mine to the storage pit (See Figure 8). I scampered up and down the ramp, fetching tools and holding planks as he cut and nailed them. When finished, the scoop ran up and down the wood ramp smoothly, and I felt good about my small role in its construction. Once set up, the mechanical loader with three miners underground could scoop sixty to eighty tons each day. Production was great and this dog-hole was safer than most. Dad and Gino received about $5 to $5.50 per ton from the breaker. Miners made $12 to $14 per day, the owner of the coal rights was paid about 50 cents per ton, and Uncle Elmo received 50 to 60 cents per ton to load the dump-truck and haul the coal to the breaker. By this time, Uncle Elmo had married Aunt Jean and the "artistic tributes" to Marilyn Monroe on the "Sistine Chapel Ceiling" of the Brockway had been removed. Dad began paying me $5 per day, and I will always recall my first paycheck of $60 for two weeks' work. Each summer, I received a $1 per day pay increase and enjoyed checking the growing balance in my bankbook every two weeks after Mother deposited my paycheck. From my perspective, life was great. I was developing a personal estate while doing exciting work with Superman! If I were born seventy years later, I probably would be spending my boyhood on an I-pad; but who knows: Perhaps that would be just as exciting as bulldozers and Brockway dump-trucks? Since I've never owned, nor will I likely ever own an I-pad or cell phone, I'll probably never know the answer to that question.

Occasionally at the end of a day's work, Dad and the other miners would meet in the basement under our restaurant and drink quarts of cold beer, which would be deducted from the miners' paychecks. I, also, would select from a case of soda pop that contained multiple flavored bottles, and Dad directed Mother to deduct the cost of the case of soda from my "estate". Reflecting back on that deduction, I realize now that I probably should have filed a labor grievance. After all, I was already mowing grass, washing the car, and daily feeding our home's coal stove and removing its' ashes, and without a weekly allowance. If I could have located "Black Jack" Kehoe, I would have joined the Molly Maguires! Of course, I joke badly (again) and cannot recall ever complaining to Dad about anything. Mother felt the same way about Dad. No one challenged Superman. However, one might argue (but not I) that as a 'drill instructor' in Anthracite Boot Camp, Dad may have been overly drilling, on occasion.

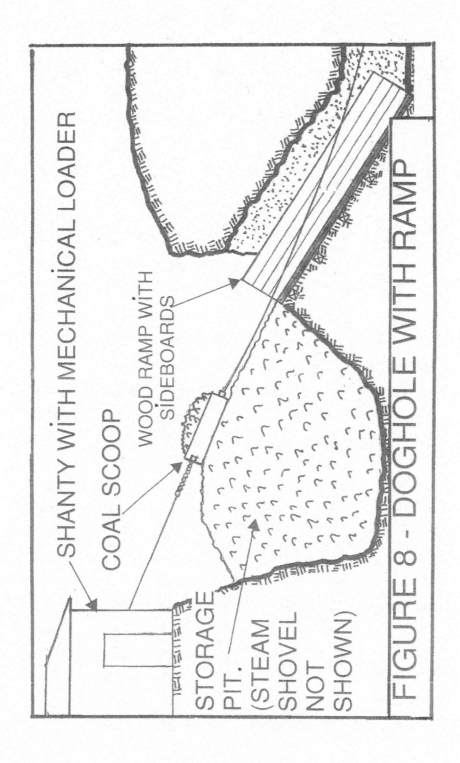

SHANTY WITH MECHANICAL LOADER

COAL SCOOP

WOOD RAMP WITH SIDEBOARDS

STORAGE PIT. (STEAM SHOVEL NOT SHOWN)

FIGURE 8 – DOGHOLE WITH RAMP

In looking back, I have fond memories of that black-faced, grimy group sitting on the concrete floor in our basement, with their backs against the foundation wall near the coal bin, laughing, joking, and washing the coal dust from their throats. Many years later, one miner, Ernie Renfer from Suscon, asked me if I remembered the small bolt of lightning that penetrated a basement window near where we were sprawled during a rainstorm outside the basement. He maintained he saw the lightning strike me. I would love to think I may have somehow been blessed and anointed by a 'blast down from Heaven'; but I concluded his vision of the event may have been distorted by the cold beer. Some of my "friends", however, have suggested it might instead have been an upward anointment from the opposite direction.

To add to Dad's good fortunes, the owner of the coal rights asked a nearby competitor to terminate their operation because the competitor's production was unsatisfactory. The competitor had built a storage tipple, installed a hoist in a shanty, and dug a "gangway" tunnel with a set of rails to the top of the tipple. A gangway is a main tunnel about eight feet wide by eight feet high. The top half of the gangway is cut through coal; but the bottom half is painstakingly cut through solid rock to provide enough height to run coal cars on a rail track. Their operation used "shakers" to bring coal horizontally out of the vein and transverse to the gangway tunnel, and drop it into the coal cars parked in the gangway below the floor of the vein. Shakers were 18" wide steel chutes that sat a foot or two above the floor of the vein. The long, horizontal chute was supported on electrically operated, vertical rocker arms that were spaced every 10 or 12 feet along the length of the horizontal chute. The shaker-chute constantly rocked back and forward, sliding the coal in the chute out to the mine car in the gangway with each sudden, forward thrust. Shakers were an old mining system that was fading away into mining history at that time because almost every pound of coal had to be hand-shoveled onto the chute. With the mechanical loader, however, the miner only had to position the scoop behind or on the side of a pile of coal, and one ton was quickly on its way out to the stockpile near the steam-shovel. Gangway, hoist, and tipple made sense when the vein was very deep and/or the mining was occurring beneath a town or developed region. There, a long tunnel made sense because a wide surface pit in a residential or commercial development wasn't possible. In remote areas, however, Dad knew that conventional gangway, hoist, and tipple did not make economic sense where shallow veins could easily, and quickly, be revealed with a bulldozer to rapidly set up and start dog-holes. Dad also concluded that underground mining made more sense economically than blasting and strip-mining the solid rock. In strip-mining, and in addition to lease payments to the owner of the rights to the coal, the mine operator also had to pay the owners of the strip-mined lands a performance bond of several thousand dollars. The mine operator would receive most of the bond payment back only if he restored the ground surface to its original condition after the strip-mining was complete.

Running the mechanical loader was a messy job. The internal drive shaft of the loader had to be lubricated periodically and after a few hours of heated operation, the drive shaft bearings began to spit hot grease at the operator. Most loader operators cut and clamped cardboard to the drums to intercept the grease 'spit', and faced with the task of washing my clothes, Mother probably wished I took time to do the same. As the steel cables in the drum became worn, they also began gradually shredding and spewing tiny steel fragments. Cardboard would have also helped to block the steel fragments. Almost all anthracite coal veins contain one or two thin, embedded seams of slate rock, which miners called "boney". As Uncle Elmo loaded each truckload with the steam-shovel, it was my job to turn off the mechanical loader, jump into the box of the dump-truck, and pitch out the boney as he rapidly loaded and dumped each bucket of coal near my feet in the truck's box. If a slab of rock was too heavy for me, my Uncle would jump up into the box of the truck and toss it out. No rock slab was too large for Uncle Elmo. Often, the switch that he depressed to release the coal from the bucket didn't function, and I had to yank on the small cable that opened the hinged door to empty the bucket. Like Dad, my Uncle worked with jinnegar, loading and turning the steam-shovel rapidly, jogging to the cab of the truck, and speeding to a breaker seven to eight miles away in Moosic or Old Forge, or five miles to the breaker in nearby Hughestown (Top of Figure 1). At times, trucks had to wait in line at the breaker before they could weigh and dump their coal. This delay was additional incentive for my Uncle to accelerate loading and hauling.

At the breaker, the weighmaster would read the scale for the weight of the coal and give my Uncle a receipt for the net weight of the coal in pounds. From his elevated position in the scale house, the weighmaster could also view and assess the quality of the coal on top of the truck, and dock the scale's measured weight by a half ton, or more, if he did not like what he saw. For this reason, it was not only necessary for me to remove boney from the truck, but also place the best coal chunks at the front of the box, or temporarily on the canopy over the truck's cab. When the truck was full, I would remove the chunks from the canopy and distribute them over the top of the load. Thus, the chunks were like the icing on a beautiful fudge cake. In this manner, not only did the coal on top of the truck look good to the weighmaster at the scale house, but shiny large chunks placed at the front of the truck's box also resulted in a "fudged dressing" on the top surface of the pile when the load was dumped into the breaker's hopper. It paid to be nice to the weighmaster. Dad and Uncle Elmo saw to it that the weighmaster received a bottle of Schenley or Old Grand Dad every Christmas.

One day, an unhappy weighmaster told my Uncle and another trucker that there was a lot of boney showing up on the conveyor to the top of the breaker, and he instructed both drivers to dump their loads on the ground near the hopper for closer examination. After dumping his coal, the other driver poked at the surface of the pile with a hand shovel, simultaneously proclaiming his load was in order. Uncle Elmo grabbed the shovel from the other driver's hands and rapidly dug down two or three feet through the 'anthracite cake fudge' to expose all the boney and undesirable material under the dressing. On some rare occasions when coal was in very great demand, however, the weighmaster's interest in quality waned, and my Uncle said it was not necessary for me to remove the boney. On some very rare occasions, he might even load a bucket of rock from the side of the storage pit, hiding it deep inside the truck box against the tailgate. By the end of the life of a dog-hole, the storage pit had often grown in size. This may appear dishonest, but I prefer to call it, "bending the truth." At that time, men continuing to emerge from the dark shadows of The Great Depression, including the weighmaster, bent it a lot.

CHAPTER VII

UNDERGROUND BOOT CAMP (1953)

Out of concern for my safety, Dad rarely instructed me to enter dog-holes; but for a few days that summer, he asked me to join him deep inside at the "face" of the mine after I had pulled that day's cut of coal out to the pit with the loader. In later years, I concluded that he felt this was a necessary chapter in my Anthracite Boot Camp training. I'm also certain he felt this particular dog-hole at Irish Hill was relatively safe. In looking back, I can say it certainly was not even as remotely treacherous as some of the other ten or twelve dog-holes that I can recall. On this day, Dad said that after we pulled out the previous cut of coal, and after I heard ten bells to turn on the electric power, I should put on a helmet and lamp, and follow the tail rope back to the mine face. Once there, I would help him set props and drill the holes for the next cut of coal. This was always done near the end of the shift so that gases from the detonation would eventually subside that evening before the miners returned to the mine the next morning. The helmet was still a little loose over my baseball cap, and with boots and elevated helmet, at age eleven, I could stand erect in the five-foot high mine, with an inch or two to spare.

As I followed the tail rope back to the miners, I reached an area where the roof and floor "pinched" close together to allow a crawl space of only about eighteen or twenty inches. I was apprehensive about wiggling through the very tight space and noticed that at some distance to the left and right, the vein seemed to be higher. However, I was afraid of inadvertently wandering off into the seemingly endless maze of black chambers and I elected, instead, to stay close to the tail-rope and crawl through the tight space. Years later, I was doubtful when a retired miner, Nunzio Massarra (Senior) of Inkerman, told me he once worked in a very low vein without being able to roll over onto his backside throughout a work shift. Not only that, but he said he once became lodged between roof and floor and had to be pulled free, feet first, by another miner! I was dis-believing until I recalled my own experience wiggling under the pinched roof in 1953, and it slowly dawned on me that what Nunzio told me was quite likely. In recent years, when my wife asks me if I had a "difficult day at the office," I think of Dad and other miners drilling, shoveling, and setting props in that pinched vein. During my current professional life in an engineering office, in response to an associate who refers to his "work", I playfully respond, *"You call this **work**?? It's certainly not like mining anthracite, especially in a pinched vein!"*

On the day of my first trip underground, I mostly walked erect for six or seven hundred feet and soon reached the mine face where I began to help Dad and Sam cut and set props. With an ax, they would hack out a small hitch (or depression) in the rock floor of the mine that was a little larger than the nine or ten-inch diameter of the round wood prop. The hitch was intended to prevent the prop from sliding on the slick floor of the mine and dis-lodging from the roof. They measured the distance from the bottom of the hitch to the roof, allowing an inch or two extra for the wood cap pieces (prop wedges) that they would sledge hammer into place to wedge the top of the prop to the roof. The "Molly Maguires" is a wonderful Hollywood movie; but the actors in the roles of the miners weakly swing sledge hammers at prop wedges, and meekly hack at coal with steel picks. The real miners that I remember had far more 'jinnegar'; but of course, they were also paid much better than the "Mollies". (For a typical view of mine props with roof wedges and floor hitches, see Figure 12.)

It took several minutes of experience with the large, very sharp, two-man saw before I learned to pull horizontally without placing any vertical weight on the handle that might otherwise force the saw down and bind it in the prop. I don't know why a power saw wasn't used; but perhaps it was prohibited by mine safety regulations at that time. Normally, it took two men to force the electric drill horizontally into the anthracite to create the eight or nine foot long drill hole. (See Figure 9 for three types of mining drills, including an electric drill.) If electricity wasn't available at the mine, a similar drill powered by compressed air from a compressor parked outside the mine was used. After several holes, the carbide drill bit attached at the end of the drill became worn, and no amount of force could push the drill through the hard anthracite. The worn drill bits had to be replaced after drilling a few holes, and Dad re-sharpened them each evening on a grinding wheel in the basement of our home. A row of ten or twelve holes, each two or three feet apart, was drilled just above the floor of the vein, and another similar row just below the roof. When the miners were standing and leaning forward over the drill, they could spread their feet so they had sufficient leverage to force the drill forward into the coal. However, the bottom row of drill holes was more difficult to drill because the miners had to push from a kneeling position. Since the nearest line of props was several feet from the face of the coal pillar, they also could not brace their feet or shoulders against the props to force the drill into the coal. At times, Dad directed me to sit on the floor

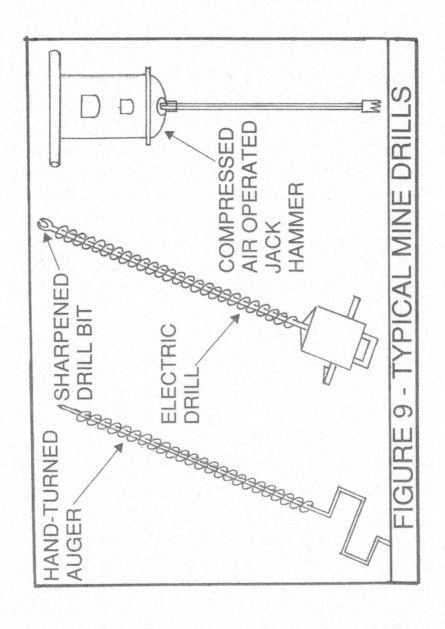

HAND-TURNED AUGER

SHARPENED DRILL BIT

ELECTRIC DRILL

COMPRESSED AIR OPERATED JACK HAMMER

FIGURE 9 - TYPICAL MINE DRILLS

with my feet braced to a prop. Then he could sit with his back to my own and push on the drill with his feet while Sam operated the switch on the drill's handle. What I would pay for that photo or painting! When I was not helping with the drill or cutting props, I would fill "tamping bags" with the coarse coal powder that the drill's rotating auger pulled out and piled on the mine floor under each drill hole. The eight or ten inch long paper tamping bags were the same two inch diameter as the drill hole, and after three or four sticks of dynamite were pushed into each hole, the tamping bags were rammed into the hole and compacted against the dynamite with a wood "tamping stick." When the dynamite was detonated later, the tamping bags forced the blast laterally into the coal seam, instead of allowing the blast force to ineffectively blow back out of the drill hole. The first stick of dynamite placed in a drill hole was embedded with a 'delay fuse' attached to a wire that extended to the exterior of the hole. Delays were in time increments of one to ten seconds so that all drill holes did not explode simultaneously with a huge force that might cause a roof collapse. Timing and coordinating each individual drill hole's burst also served to neatly "peal away" the coal from the solid rib of the vein, much like one would sequentially peal an orange with their thumb.

Miners referred to the practice of angling and spacing drill holes, inserting the right amount of dynamite, and selecting the correct delay fuses, as "cutting coal", and considered it an important art in coal mining. When done "artfully" by a skilled miner, the bottom row would be timed to explode first, then the top row timed to bring the overhanging portion down in chunks. Coal had to be "cut" properly to prevent delivery of excessively powdered material, which the weighmaster might dock from the real measured weight. The correct amount of dynamite also had to be carefully estimated to prevent the coal from scattering among the props. The drill holes had to also be oriented to force the resulting coal pile to accumulate where it would be more easily accessible to the scoop. Occasionally after the detonation, a thick seam of coal remained clinging semi-tightly to the smooth rock roof. With a heavy steel pinch bar, the miner would pry the seam of coal down from the roof, and hopefully, without bringing any part of the roof down on top of him.

After drilling and charging the drill holes with dynamite was complete, I followed the tail rope back outside to the shanty. Sixty-seven years later, I can still picture the huge grin on Uncle Elmo's face when, from his seat in the steam-shovel, he saw his blackened, eleven year-old nephew with oversized helmet crawling up the wood ramp. Upon entering the shanty, I turned off the power and disconnected the wire to the mine at the wall-mounted fuse box so the miners could safely connect the wire at their end to the dynamite in the drill holes. In recent years, I've come to marvel at the level of trust to which the miners placed their personal safety in the hands of an eleven-year old boy. However, as I light-heartedly reminded my wife, "Perhaps they knew the boy was gifted???"

After the miners emerged from the mine, I reconnected the wire and threw the lever on the fuse box to detonate the drill holes. The ground shook in a series of seven or eight explosions that occurred in one or two-second intervals, in the same sequence set with the delayed timing fuses. On another rare occasion, I worked inside the mine while another miner operated the mechanical loader. I would touch the ends of the bell wires together whenever Dad said to stop or start the scoop, and I managed all signals out to the loader operator in the shanty as Dad directed. At one point, Dad and I were on our knees shoveling coal side by side and he asked me, "*Why did you stop?*" I responded that, "*I have a headache.*" To this day, I can recall I didn't make it up as an excuse, and can also recall exactly how Dad responded. He hesitated momentarily while planning his response, and then softly said, "*Don't you think I have one too?*" I know that I could not have been a very productive miner at age eleven, and after recalling his diplomatic response, it is clear to me that Dad was very focused on developing my work ethic. One would have to ask that, in addition to all he had to endure under severe working conditions underground, why would Dad want to further burden himself with such additional effort to train a young son?? The miner behind the loader in the shanty could have substantially reduced Dad's burden if the miner and I switched places. It was a burden and effort by Dad that I shall **always** respect and honor.

Among the small mining operations during that period, con- tractual agreements between mine owners were mostly unwritten, and conflicts of interests were common. The legal profession at that time was far less widespread than it is today, now that every small borough in The Wyoming Valley seems to have a law office in every shopping plaza. "Contractor Reprisals" of the type that follows were not very uncommon. One weekend, we were walking along a remote dirt road near a mine operated by another competitor. The competitor's equip- ment was parked nearby and no one was around. Dad began describing to me how I should proceed down the road and swing through the woods to flush out any deer toward where he would be posted on a hilltop with the Fox shotgun. I proceeded down the road for only a few minutes when I heard a series of six or seven blasts from the shotgun. I ran back as fast as I could to where Dad was standing and saw the windows of the mine equipment were shattered, tires were flat, and water was leaking from the radiators. I looked at Dad and, bewildered, said nothing. With what I distinctly remember as a 'look of apology', he solemnly said to me, "*They owed us $4,000 and refused to pay.*" I often recall the event as remindful of the classic Hollywood movie and Don Corleone in Part I of "*The Godfather*". The Don was usually honorable;

but not always lawful. Sometimes, contract reprisals in the form of nasty hits were justified, or so it seemed to the Don and his family. For me, personally, the deep mellow voice of Al Martino performing the classic movie's theme song, *"SPEAK SOFTLY"*, interpreted the "nasty hits" in a manner that transparently communicated fairness and justification for the reprisal. Although the intense strife that existed in the anthracite coal fields thirty or forty years earlier had dissipated, it was obvious that occasional small vendettas still persisted.

On another occasion around the same time, Dad sold his bulldozer to another company who discontinued payments after a few months. Dad went to that company's mine early one Sunday morning and drove the dozer down a steep riverbank, and as in an old Western movie, continued up the Lackawanna River a substantial distance from that mine to hide his tracks. There, he steered the dozer back up the steep river bank and loaded it on a truck for the return trip to his mine. A court judge later ruled that the other company had to legally return the dozer to Dad, and Dad had to return the other company's few initial payments. Dad and Gino also experienced material theft at their own dog-holes often, and I can recall Dad working with the Dupont Chief of Police, Frank Palumbo, to address the problem. Occasionally, supplies and equipment were missing; but coal theft from the stockpile was more common. After a series of visits by coal thieves, Dad hid at the mine late one evening, waiting for the culprits to return. After threatening them with the Fox shotgun, the two intruders took off and never returned.

CHAPTER VIII

THE NEW BOSTON MINE (1954)

Dad had a playful way of waking me in the morning for work if I lingered in bed. Typically, he would have a shot of whiskey with his morning black coffee, especially during the bitter cold winters that were quite common to Northeastern Pennsylvania. He would stir his forefinger in a cup of the concoction near my bed and silently spread it along my lips. I could still see that big grin on his face as he retreated through the door, confident that I would be along shortly. The "grin out the door" always reminded me of Nonna's "grin out the door" the evening of her prank in Old Boston after she "treated" me with homemade red wine. Often, I would also be a little slow joining Dad in the pickup for the drive to the mine. He typically would begin edging down the driveway without saying a word, forcing me to run quickly to catch up with him about 100-200 feet from the house. Dad had a very effective way of communicating with me without saying much, and without words of anger. In the same respect, he also did not say much when he made every effort to show me a good time. Examples were the three or four times Dad, Uncle Elmo, Gino, and I made the three-hour car trip to Yankee Stadium to see the New York Yankees in Sunday doubleheaders. Prior to one doubleheader, the waitress in the restaurant across from the stadium rudely and loudly announced, "*I guess this is mine,"* as she pocketed the remaining cash as her tip after Dad paid her for our lunch. She probably knew from experience that she could take advantage of polite coal miners from The Wyoming Valley, and that anthracite miners weren't the best tippers in New York. As was his nature, Dad did not raise an objection to her; but the experience was the topic of humorous conversation in the car a number of times during the return trip home. The other memorable topic was the lightning speed Mickey Mantle displayed running from first base to home plate, despite failing his army induction physical due to bad knees. I can still see Mickey, who was my hero away from the mines, flying around the bases after a double by Moose Skowron.

Besides the thrill of Yankee Stadium, there were countless other experiences that Dad shared with me away from the mine. Examples were the countless visits to the Old Boston Italian Citizen's Club, where miners were quick to tell the bartender, *"Give the boy a birch beer or candy bar."* During bocce matches, the clubhouse was as loud and excited as any professional major league stadium packed with football or baseball fans. When a player tossed a bocce thirty feet through the air, and squarely smacked away his opponent's bocce, the group erupted in a frenzy as if the great NFL fullback, Jim Brown, had just dashed eighty yards for a touchdown. In a unified outburst, **"SAY'-CO-SAY- EE!"** literally meant, "Air bomb the opponent's bocce and replace it with the striker's own bocce bomb right near the small paulino, and close to two of the striker's other nearby bocce's, for a total of six points". At other times, yelling **"CO-STA-CO-STA!"** meant, "Roll the bocce slowly up to the small paulino". A loud **"STR'EESH!"** meant, "Roll the bocce hard and knock the opponent's bocce out of the way". These were very loud outbursts intended to guide the thrown bocce, and could be heard all over Old Boston from the club-house, which was somewhat centered in the mining settlement. In the game of **"MORRA"** (pronounced "**MOD-A**"), a group of 6 or 8 miners stood in a circle as two opposing players simultaneously yelled their predicted sum of fingers displayed at the instant both opponents slammed their right hands forward. Yelling their guesses, such as, "**QUA'- TRO!**"(Four), "**DU- EE!**" (Two), or "**OTT'- OO!**" (Eight), etc., as loud as possible, seemed part of the game, and intended to intimidate their opponent. After an hour, the fatigued and hoarse group had to retreat to the bar and cold beer to regain their voices. The club-house and 'joo-go' (bocce court) are no longer there; but I can easily recall the passion of the previous generations of miners whenever I make my annual visit from Arizona, and walk Old Boston Road along its' two-mile length.

There were, also, baseball practices on the huge lawn of the Comerford Drive-in Theater on Highway 315, across the highway from our home and restaurant. There, Dad seemed to enjoy hitting fly balls to me, and Uncle Armando (Army) Scatena sometimes participated in the hitting as well. On one occasion in Dad's absence, Uncle Army hit a long fly ball beyond the edge of the Theater's lawn, and into the adjacent wild brush. While focused on the ball high in the sky, I ran into the woods beyond the edge of the lawn, and fell into a six- foot deep ravine filled with needle bushes. Laying on my back, I can still picture the huge fiery grin on my Uncle's face as he ran fast up to the edge of the hole. Looking down to where I lay in the brush with 5 or 6 wood needles embedded a half inch in my arms, he yelled very excitedly, "**DID YOU CATCH IT? DID YOU CATCH IT?**" It was one small and typical example how Uncle Army, just like Dad and Uncle Elmo, focused intensely on performance and production, with little regard for personal safety.

There were also countless hunting expeditions and fishing trips with Dad, Sam, and my uncles once I was old enough to have a license. I don't think I ever could sleep in the evening before a hunting trip. Early one Sunday morning, Dad took me to Suscon on a fishing excursion to the very remote, north end of the Big Dam. We turned off Suscon Road onto Chapel Road and traveled about three miles south on a very potholed dirt road to an unoccupied hunting shack that Dad called "Pinchko's Cabin." We parked the pickup and walked a worn path for about one-half mile. Not a single soul was anywhere to be seen or heard. I carried the fishing equipment, as Dad led the way, 'at the ready' with his Fox double-barrel. When we reached the point where Mill Creek flows into the reservoir, Dad suddenly swung the 12 gage "Fox fishing rod" from his shoulder and blasted a large pickerel for the "catch-of-the day". Dad was forever a determined hunter, and not a patient fisherman; but what happened on the path before we reached the creek was far more bizarre. It was only minutes before daybreak and a creepy mist enveloped the surrounding thick forest. As usual, Dad was on the hunt and the air was so silent that even a leaf hitting the ground probably could be heard. As I walked quietly on the path six or seven feet behind him carrying my fishing pole and bucket, we suddenly heard a slow, rhythmic 'thumping' that grew louder as it accelerated to a very rapid frequency. Then, the strange sound very rapidly faded away three or four seconds later. Dad yanked the shotgun off his shoulder and stared intently into the mist; but resumed walking a minute later. The "bizarre" part was that I knew the sudden thumping that we both heard was not coming out of the dense woods; but instead, emanated from........ **within my own eardrums!** Yes, I was (and am) very certain of it; but I was too startled to mention such a strange and crazy experience to him.

Thanks to the Internet, I learned recently that there is such an ear defect called "Objective Pulsatile Tinnitus," which I never again experienced. Perhaps the event was not so crazy, after all. Again, thanks to the Internet, Tinnitis may even explain my tendency to substantial motion sickness on amusement rides when I was at that age and a little older. In retrospect, I have also wondered if the continuous ear-piercing blast that I experienced around that time, as I sat against a huge dragline diesel engine in an effort to stay warm on a frigid winter day, may have led to the Tinnitus. After all, today's industrial safety rules and regulations prevent even mature workers from positioning themselves near such noisy equipment without ear protection. Gradually and thankfully, my problem with motion sickness slowly dissipated over the years that followed. In fact, a much-appreciated benefit of Tinnitus may have cropped up recently. After I failed to heed one of her (many) orders, my wife of fifty-seven years admonished, "*I think you're losing your hearing*," to which I pleasantly and happily responded, **"THAT'S GREAT NEWS! I CAN'T WAIT!"** I also enjoy poking a little fun her way whenever I laughingly open a sales letter in the mail that advertises a hearing aid.

One Monday morning following a trip to Yankee Stadium, Dad emerged from the mine as I was running the mechanical loader, and casually said he had to go "some place". The rain jacket draped over his arm seemed a little odd; but nothing appeared wrong. When the miners emerged at the end of the day, I learned "some place" was the hospital, and the rain jacket hid a fractured and bleeding wrist from me. A sudden lurch of the scoop had jammed his wrist to the roof of the mine. When I arrived home that evening, Dad said he knew he was placing his arm in a dangerous position between the moving scoop and the roof of the mine; but the lack of sleep after returning from one of our long trips to Yankee Stadium clouded his better judgment.

At this time, Dad and Gino started a mine on the outskirts of the small mining settlement of New Boston, which is one mile north of Old Boston, two miles south of Dupont, and on the east side of State Highway 315. I helped Dad drill and blast the rock to develop the pit and reveal the vein. Each of us operated a compressed air jackhammer to drill vertically down into rock that was about thirty feet thick over the coal. (See the third drill in Figure 9 for a jackhammer.) I would love to brag that I manhandled the heavy jackhammer; but it weighed approximately ninety pounds and had to be lifted and steadied about six feet above the drill hole. Dad would leave his jackhammer, start each drill hole for me, turn the jackhammer over to me to operate, and then return to his own jackhammer. One day, he positioned me far from the drill holes and detonated the thirty or forty dynamite-filled drill holes with a blasting plunger, while crouching under a truck-mounted air compressor. A rock about the size of a soft ball bounced under the truck and struck him just above the knee. Fortunately, the injury was not serious; but he limped for several days on a severely swollen leg. Such injuries were quite common among miners and if they were very lucky, they might only experience a few broken bones during their mining career. Dad experienced numerous similar injuries; but I never heard so much as, **"OW"**!

The vein in New Boston was about 4-1/2 feet thick and the mine sloped down to the west under Highway 315. Dad pushed as hard as ever. As Uncle Elmo loaded the truck at the pit, Dad could often hear the distant rumbling of the steam-shovel echoing back into the mine. As soon as he heard the echoing die away, he knew I was through pitching boney off the truck, and sounded the bell in the shanty to signal me to re-start the loader. A few seconds later as Uncle Elmo pulled away and I scurried up the side of the pit to the shanty, he would ring the bell again, and again 3 or 4 seconds later. Although he was quite stern, Dad never once raised a hand to me and hardly ever had to yell. As soon as I heard his message, I moved. He would often call out, **"RUN, DON'T WALK**!" Forty years later, Uncle Gildo's wife, Aunt Dorthea, said she could still picture me, "Running non-stop under Dad's direction", many years after she had observed Dad and I working around our home. However, just think about it: isn't that the way *anyone* would respond to "Superman"?

I had become quite proficient in the operation of the mechanical loader and Dad also began to give me opportunities to operate the Caterpillar bulldozer, which was similar to the one shown in Figure 10. One day, he instructed me to drive it about two miles up a dirt road from Yatesville (Center of Figure 1), across Highway 315, and an additional one-half mile to the doghole in New Boston. Running the big dozer down the dirt road was exhilarating, especially after I threw it into third gear.

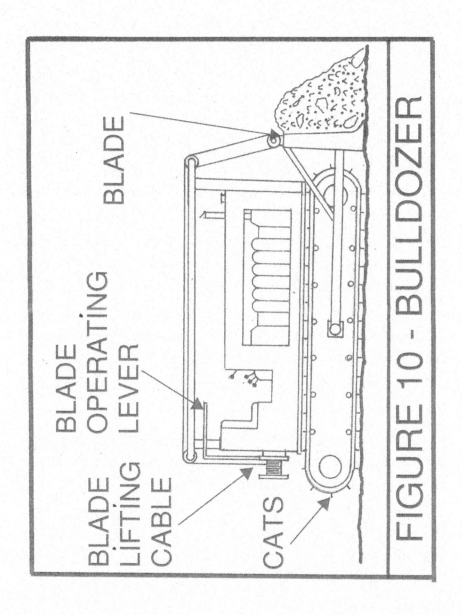

FIGURE 10 – BULLDOZER

Dad was waiting for me when I arrived on the west side of Highway 315 with the dozer. He stopped the traffic and placed wood planks on the pavement so the dozer's steel cats would not damage the highway. Then, he removed the planks and continued on to other business after I crossed the highway. As I was going down a dirt road in New Boston, I was very nervous because the wide blade on the front of the dozer barely fit between the wire fences that lined the yards of private homes on each side of the dirt road. As the dozer crawled along near one of the homes, an elderly woman followed alongside, yelling and waving her arms at me frantically, and crying very tearfully at the same time. I was be-wildered, had no idea what upset her, or what I should do, and I just continued guiding the dozer past her. I learned much later that the lady's name was Mrs. Pascucci. Apparently, her husband was extremely ill in bed, upset by the roar of the ground-shaking dozer, and died days or weeks later. It wasn't until I was many years older that it dawned on me that I should have at least turned the throttle way down, or perhaps even stop to try to help the poor lady. In recent years, the homes have been replaced by a large warehouse complex and the little anthracite coal mining village of New Boston no longer exists.

I also wanted to try my hand at operating the steam-shovel. One day, I asked an impatient dump-truck driver if he would like me to load his truck so he didn't have to wait any longer for Uncle Elmo to arrive and load it for him. I had never operated a steam-shovel before; but I assured him I knew 'how' when he asked me if I could. I can still see the mouth-open, look of alarm on the driver's face as he glared up at the side of his truck box, when I (lightly) banged it with the steam-shovel's bucket.

Now that I was a little older, my fear of bears and snakes around the shanty was replaced by a touch of boredom. On one occasion, I stepped onto the top of the loader, gripped the rafters of the shanty to balance myself, and attempted to operate the two levers of the loader with my feet. I am most certain Dad was not at the mine that day, and thankfully, no miners ever spotted me. I discontinued that dangerous practice within a few days. I also got into a little trouble when I decided to playfully drive Dad's pickup back and forth on the dirt road leading to the mine, while he and the other miners were underground. As he drove home late that afternoon, I slumped down in my seat, and began to lose my breath, when I noticed Dad intensely examining the fresh tire tracks zig-zagging up and down the side of the hill along the dirt road. I froze as, out of the corner of my eye, I watched his puzzled expression gradually turn to anger. It slowly dawned on him that the imprint of fresh tire tracks running up and down the steep side slopes of the dirt road were the treads of his own pickup! It was the last time I drove his pickup without his permission.

One day, Dad said that the State Mine Inspector would be paying us a visit that week, and I should keep my eyes open for any unidentifiable cars coming up the dirt road. When I saw the vehicle, I was to sneak out the small wall opening through which the mechanical loader's cables passed, and innocently sit some distance away from the shanty. Unfortunately, the inspector spotted me sneaking out the opening as he drove up the road. After he got out of his car, he said angrily, *"I saw you sneaking out of the shanty! Get your father out of the mine!"* When Dad emerged from the mine, he sat quietly outside the entrance of the mine as the inspector proceeded to chew him out. He threatened Dad with severe penalties for violating child labor laws, and that was the end of my mining career,……….. for about two or three weeks at that dog-hole. The original notification by the inspector of his pending visit also alerted Dad to the hasty need to add some mine props in certain locations, to help ensure successful passage of the inspection. Apparently, prevailing protocol by state and federal mine inspectors during that period of time could have been improved.

At the New Boston mine, I witnessed another sight I will never forget. I followed Gino down to the mine entrance; but I myself had no need or intention to enter the dog-hole. As I sat on the ground near the entrance, Gino looked up at the roof just before crawling into the mine and yelled, *"Wait, kid! Back up! We're going to have a little excitement!"* I instantly glanced up at the exposed edge of the roof surface and I could see the surface of the rock rapidly cracking and "checker boarding". In the very short span of two or three seconds, I watched the cracks in the roof proliferate and widen rapidly until about three or four tons of rock suddenly crashed to the floor of the mine, just a few feet in front of us. Undoubtedly, the vague sound and sight of such fracturing is what mine rats sense just before running out of a mine that is about to collapse. On that day, Gino climbed over the rock pile laughing and, as he descended the slope into the mine, was singing improvised lyrics about how his *"worthless life isn't worth a plugged nickel"*. I often heard miners talk about the importance of keeping an eye on the roof as they traveled and worked underground; but the chance of fore-seeing the beginning of a roof collapse in poorly lit mine chambers strikes me as being extremely unlikely. Nevertheless, the precautionary practice paid off 'big time' for Gino, and perhaps for me, on that particular day.

As much as I admired them, miners frequently made me the target of their jokes, as they did when they imitated a bear chasing me. Gino once laughingly asked me, in very explicit (and unprintable) terms that I had never heard before, something about the extent of my sexual experience with women. At age thirteen, I only knew that women existed, and that they were suspiciously different from men. His exact words, as I (much) later learned, were quite raunchy, even in

Anthracite Boot Camp. When I went home that evening puzzled by his comments, I quoted Gino and asked Mother, *"What did Gino mean?"* She became extremely upset and strongly admonished that I should never use those words again. The next day, Gino said Dad had angrily complained to him, and Gino shook his head in total amazement at my acute lack of awareness in this subject. Gino was a great icon and like an Uncle to me. To this day, I greatly regret my question to my Mother, whatever the question was, and how badly my ignorance must have hurt her and Gino.

About the same time, I again found myself in a similar position of embarrassment. One day, the mechanical loader was silent because Dad and two other miners were setting props and attending to other 'dead work'. Since they were only about 100 feet inside, I went down and sat near the mine entrance to pass time listening to the conversations as they worked. One miner was bragging about a recent conquest in bed with some woman. I sat there and listened intently, without understanding any of it, as he shared all of the most intimate details with Dad and another miner. At that instant, Dad suddenly suspected there might be an unexpected listener, hushed the miner, and subtly called out my name. After I responded hesitantly, the mine suddenly fell silent, except for the clanking of the shovels and saws. On another day, Dad and Sam were talking about Sam's hunting dog, Snowball, and I naively interrupted them with, *"How can you tell if a dog is a boy or a girl?"* While both were laughing profusely at my question, Sam responded, *"You pick it up by the tail and smell it!"* When they were through laughing, Sam said, *"Someday, I'm going to tell you a little secret about boys and girls that's going to leave you with your mouth wide open and in shock!"* To say that I was naïve on this particular subject would be a gross understatement. Using a slang expression often heard from my Italian ancestors to describe a grossly unaware and backward person, I was probably a "Gnocco" (Nee - oo'- cho), which literally translates to, "A Potato Dumpling". It may also suggest that although Gnocchi was always my favorite dish of pasta, I may have consumed too much of it. Perhaps spending so much of my youth at anthracite dog-holes also contributed indirectly to my apparent underdevelopment in the social arena; but more about that topic in an upcoming chapter.

CHAPTER IX

THE EXETER MINE (1955)

The location of this mine was near the base of the mountain on the west side of the Wyoming Valley, and about 1/4 mile southwest of the Fox Hill Country Club and Golf Course in West Pittston (Upper left corner in Figure 1). Here, down within the low point of the Valley, below the surface of existing farms, Dad mined the thickest, most beautiful vein of anthracite I had ever seen. Of all Dad's dog-holes, this was probably the only one down deep in the Valley at a distance from the anthracite vein outcrops that were higher up on the mountain sides. I can't recall if this one in Exeter mined into the Clark, Marcey, Checker, Red Ash, or one of the other officially mapped anthracite veins; but it was magnificent, indeed. It was extremely hard anthracite, and when two chunks bumped, it made a sound very similar to the sound that two empty coke bottles make when bumped together lightly, hence, the anthracite nickname, "Bottle Coal." Unfortunately, there was one major drawback with this bonanza that was not apparent when Dad first placed his dragline on the existing farmland and began digging down to the vein, i.e., **GROUNDWATER!** The exact location on the east side of Slocum Avenue has since been developed for private homes, and was what would now be near the present intersection of Holly Lane and Daisy Court streets. The pit was, and still partially remains, in a low-lying area, and runoff from surrounding hills during rainstorms found, and continues to find its way to this location. With his dragline, Dad excavated a pit about 150 feet square and 50 feet deep into the farm soil, which was above the 10 or 15 feet of solid roof rock that covered the rich vein. (See Figure 11 for a dragline similar to Dad's.) Then, heavy rains saturated The Wyoming Valley. The surface farm soil was loose and a sub-surface stream about six feet below the surface emerged through the pit wall, and was filling the pit with water. Dad traced the course of the hidden stream to a point about 200 feet to the south where the water was passing below the surface, and through a shallow layer of loose, crushed mine rock left by a colliery that once operated nearby. With the dragline at the location of the sub-surface stream, he dug a trench through the loose mine rock and down to the underlying firm clay. The trench was about 8 feet wide by 6 feet deep and 50 feet long to expose the sub-surface stream below the loose rock. As he dug the trench, Dad dumped the rock as far as the dragline could reach; however, he directed me to push it even further away with the caterpillar dozer. At one point, I turned the caterpillar sideways on a steep side slope, where the dozer felt ready to topple on its' side if I moved another foot forward or back, and so I stopped and froze. On this rare occasion, Dad was annoyed with me and yelled, "*What the hell are you doing? Are you trying to tip it over?*" He straightened the machine out and I learned another valuable lesson in Anthracite Boot Camp.

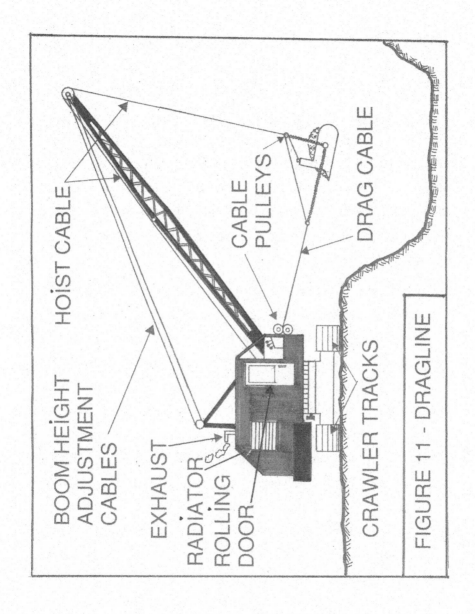

FIGURE 11 - DRAGLINE

At the bottom of the trench that Dad excavated, the stream was exposed and flowing on firm clay. With the dragline, Dad cast farm soil in the trench in approximately 12" thick, even layers. He then leveled and compacted each layer in succession with the bulldozer to build an impervious clay cut-off wall to stop the flow of the sub-surface water to the mine pit. To this day, I marvel at Dad's creative intelligence and skill in developing such makeshift technical solutions, which trained engineers might take years to learn. The lightweight, geometrically crafted mine scoop was one previous example. Now, the resulting clay cut-off wall was impervious to the stream, and flow into the mine pit two-hundred feet away ceased; but the mine pit was now three-fourth's filled with water. The average guy likely would have rented a large pump for several days to remove the water from the pit; but Dad wasn't the average guy.

The next day, after cutting off the flow of water to the pit, Dad borrowed an unusual hand auger from someone. I had never seen one like it before, and it resembled a carpenter's brace and bit used to manually bore a hole through wood(See Figure 9). However, this particular drill had a very large crank, which two miners standing face-to-face could push and pull to rotate the auger so it could bore ten or twelve feet horizontally into the vein of anthracite. No doubt, it was the type of manual drill used by miners before electric drills were invented, and Dad did not yet have electric power at this site. Dad and I entered an old abandoned mine tunnel in a wooded area about eight hundred feet east of the pit and three hundred feet south of Packer Avenue and the present-day Fox Hill Country Club Golf Course. It certainly was the nearest Dad ever got to a golf course or country club. I did not have a helmet or headlamp, and I followed him underground to a point inside the abandoned mine that he estimated was below his water-filled strip-mine. We faced each other so that my right hand was on one crank handle near his left hand, and my left hand was on the other crank handle near his right hand. As we cranked together, the auger advanced laterally and upward to my right and it took, perhaps, one or two hours to drill and insert dynamite in three holes. The vein and existing coal pillars were six feet high; but standing on loose coal or rock, my head rubbed the sandstone roof. Water was dripping from the roof and obviously originating in the water-filled pit above us that we wanted to drain. My red hunting cap was covered with muck. Miners often referred to a mucky roof as "soapstone." Dad was perturbed that I was ruining a perfectly good hunting cap, but realized it was unavoidable. He packed the drill holes with extra high explosive dynamite, which he referred to as "gelatin," and ran a wire from the exploder caps in the dynamite, and out toward the mine entrance. The wire ended one hundred to one hundred and fifty feet short of the mine entrance. Of course, the underground effects of the blast and gushing water were unpredictable. Therefore, Dad led me outside the mine, before returning back inside to the end of the wire to detonate the drill holes with a twist battery.

When we checked the pit, it was obvious the explosion failed to burst through the sandstone roof, and the pit was still full of water. The next day, however, after all the gases from the explosion cleared, Dad returned back into the abandoned mine to where we had drilled, and he filled the blasted cavity under the mine roof with more gelatin. The resulting explosion burst through the floor of the pit and drained the water from the pit, and into the abandoned mine. The next step was even more difficult than the previous one, because the clay mud now had to be removed from the drained pit. When such excavation occurs underground, miners refer to it as "mucking". In the process of excavating the muck with the dragline, the bucket, which was capable of lifting three or four tons, sank deeply into the mud and became immovable. The dragline did not have enough weight or power to lift, drag, or free the embedded bucket from the muck. Again, the average guy would likely rent a mobile crane service to free the bucket, but such a delay wasn't Dad's way.

Instead, Dad turned the front of the crawler tracks so they were pointing toward the pit, and so that the machine's heavy counterweight was over-hanging the back end of the crawler tracks. He then tensioned and locked the vertical hoisting cable so that the vertical resistance of the mired bucket lifted and held the back end of the dragline's crawler tracks about three or four feet off the ground. (See Figure 11A). By this process, the ninety-four ton weight of the tipped dragline was applying constant lift to the bucket through the vertical hoist cable, while Dad also pulled on the bucket horizontally with the drag cable. In effect, he was attempting to, simultaneously, vertically lift, and horizontally drag, the bucket out of the mud. When he tried to pull the bucket forward, however, it wouldn't budge. The front end of the crawler treads only slid closer to the edge of the deep pit, and the back end of the crawler treads crashed back down to the ground surface. Then Dad would re-apply vertical lift to the bucket to again lift the rear end of both crawler tracks off the ground, and again pull the drag cable horizontally forward, in another attempt to simultaneously lift and drag the bucket free, as shown in Figure 11A. Dad repeated this same dangerous technique numerous times; but the bucket wouldn't budge and the front edge of the crawler tracks slid closer to the edge of the pit each time. Instead of sitting in the operator's seat as he fought with the controls, he stood erect, prepared to jump off if the machine suddenly slid or toppled into the pit. To add to my fear, the cab door on the tipped dragline kept sliding forward and clanging shut so that he had to reopen it each time in order to keep his emergency escape route clear. For at least an hour, Dad ferociously battled with the dragline and its' sunken bucket.

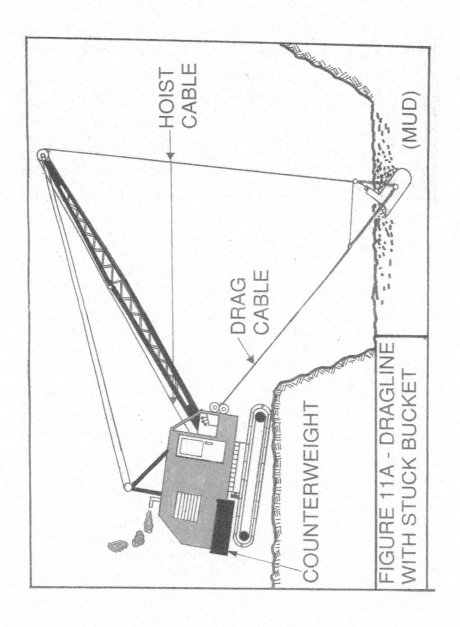

HOIST CABLE

DRAG CABLE

(MUD)

COUNTERWEIGHT

FIGURE 11A - DRAGLINE WITH STUCK BUCKET

Now, in the years I worked with Dad, I never once heard him utter a single profane curse word, that is, in English. When a machine did not do what he wanted, however, his Italian threats to the demons inside the machine streamed like the Susquehanna River. On this day, his unforgettable flow of vocal blasts was something about, "**SAN TREE-STEE- ME-TROY-YA!**", or the "**PU-TAN-NA-DE-LA-TROY-YA!**", or similar, **POC-CA-PU-TAN-NAS!**" It sounded like a Giacomo Puccini Opera, but as he knew and intended, I did not understand one single word of it. However, I was quite certain that the lyrics weren't from "LA BOHEME" or "TOSCA". Besides, Dad's anger with the stubborn and mean dragline bucket in the mud hole was in sharp contrast to Rudolpho's tenderness toward the beautiful, but ill-stricken Mimi in their one-room attic apartment in Paris during "LA BOHEME". As Dad battled with the dragline's controls, alternatively glaring down at the mired bucket, and back up at the blue sky, the outburst of volcanic lyrics was nonstop, and I froze in bewildered anticipation of disaster. The climatic gunfight music of "*THE ECSTASY OF GOLD*" composed by Ennio Morricone, and performed by Susanna Rigacci, is far more accurately interpretive of the earth-shaking battle than "LA BOHEME". The sun was directly above the machine and I most certainly had a dazed, mouth-open expression, as I squinted into the bright sunlight toward the steeply tipped dragline pivoted at the edge of the deep pit. Dad interrupted his barrage of "putannas" briefly to turn to me in the midst of his battle and yelled, "*What the hell are you laughing at?*" In retrospect, I feel quite strongly that Dad knew very well that I wasn't laughing; but even in such a dangerous predicament, my sense now is that he suddenly felt compelled to share a little heartfelt humor. Rest assured, I never found this scene the least bit amusing. I have read many books about World War II in the Pacific; but to me, Dad's long vicious battle with the tipped dragline made Iwo

Jima in February, 1945 look like a boy scout troop picnic. At the high point of Dad's Putanna concert, just as Ennio and Susanna reached their chilling, climatic crescendo in "**The Ecstasy of Gold**", the bucket broke free from the muck. Later, once the coal pillars were uncovered and coal shipped to the breaker, a certain amount of mud content was inevitable. Thus, the weighmaster's dockage on the coal's true weight was nearly as brutal as Dad's "putanna attack" on the hellish demons in the mud-hole. I recall the reduction in estimated weight was on the order of twenty to thirty percent.

Draglines struck me as being nearly as dangerous as dog-holes. Once when Dad was slowly driving the huge and awkward machine up a steep hill, he would swing the bucket ahead up the hill and dig the bucket into the dirt (See Figure 11B). Then, pulling on the embedded bucket with the drag cable, the heavy dragline could both "crawl and pull" itself up the steep incline. Once the machine crawled up to the dug-in bucket, and as the bucket continued to anchor the dragline steadfastly at that temporary location, the crawler tracks needed to be locked to prevent the straining dragline from shooting back downhill when the anchored bucket was subsequently lifted out of the dirt. Then, after he swung and dug the bucket in again uphill, the tracks had to again be unlocked so the dragline could resume its' uphill "crawl and pull". Two brake levers that looked like large sledgehammers were located underneath the counterweight, between the crawler treads, at the rear of the dragline. (See Figure 11B for their location.) I was the only guy (boy) available to repeatedly lock and unlock the brakes as the dragline crawled and struggled up the hill. I had to crawl under the dragline's counterweight, and beneath the roaring engine of the slanted dragline on the hillside, in order to flip these crawler brake locks down and up, each time Dad stopped and restarted the long "crawl and pull" up-hill. Ennio and Susanna can again perform "Ecstacy of Gold" to help one sense the pending disaster. In retrospect, other than the chase by the 'hungry black bear' on Irish Hill, the dragline hill climb was my most fearful assignment throughout Anthracite Boot Camp. You had to be with me beneath the screaming and straining dragline on the side of the steep hill to fully appreciate my fear. However, I completed my task and helped Dad crawl/pull the dragline over the top of the steep hill, just as Ennio and Susanna's "Ecstacy of Gold" reached its' chilling and climatic crescendo, again.

Dad and Gino experienced two dragline accidents during the 1950s. On the mountainside west of Old Forge, a brand-new dragline ran out of control down a hillside, toppled, and the operator from Old Forge had a serious back injury. This was precisely the type of accident that I helped Dad avoid at the Exeter mine with the crawler brake 'lock and unlock' technique. At a colliery in Keystone, two miles south of Laflin, the operator from Keystone jumped clear and escaped uninjured when the dragline toppled into a deep ravine.

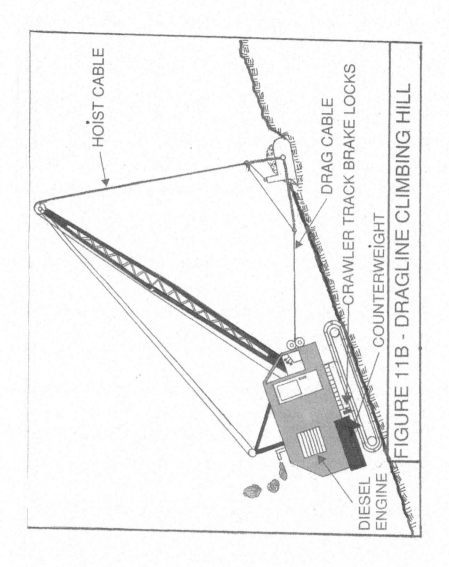

HOIST CABLE

DRAG CABLE

CRAWLER TRACK BRAKE LOCKS

COUNTERWEIGHT

DIESEL ENGINE

FIGURE 11B - DRAGLINE CLIMBING HILL

In another scenario, at the New Boston mine pit on the east side of Highway 315, the tall boom of the dragline swung back and forth only two or three feet under high voltage electrical transmission lines that still cross the highway near that location today. In order to escape the freezing temperatures one winter day, I huddled inside the cab next to the warm engine, as Dad dug the pit and swung the boom back and forth under the transmission lines. Seated under the high voltage lines seemed like a dangerous way to stay warm without frying. However, as mentioned in the previous chapter, the potential risk of Pulsatile Tinnitis on young eardrums, seated without earplugs next to that screaming diesel engine, should have been a greater concern. Additionally, I often wondered how Dad knew the steep side-slopes of pits were strong enough to support the heavy weight of the ninety-four ton machine only two or three feet from the edge of the deep pit. After all, Dad was super-intelligent, but not a trained geotechnical engineer. In general, mining equipment of that era tended to be unsafe compared to the newer technology available today. One can go online and view numerous classic photos of toppled, crumpled draglines at deep strip mines.

For three or four months at the Exeter mine, bottle coal production with the mechanical loader in the six-foot high vein was outstanding. The miners were now "robbing" old, existing coal pillars, which was very productive because the cable pulley at the back of the mine could be easily located to position the scoop behind a blasted coal pillar. However, it was also very dangerous because the roof of the mine typically squeezed downward gradually as supporting pillars were robbed or reduced in size. Many years ago, an elderly, retired miner once proudly boasted to me how he saved time and money by working under a gently descending roof as coal spalled off the face of squeezing pillars, thereby eliminating the need to drill and blast the coal. At first, I thought his story was more boastful than factual because I had never heard of this very dangerous mining technique. Then I recalled a scene in "The Molly Maguires" when a miner collected his pay at the end of a work week. The role of the miner was played by Hollywood star, Richard Harris. The miner's gross pay was sixty-six cents for each of the fourteen mine cars that he loaded. Then, five dollars and thirty cents for blasting powder and broken drills was deducted from the nine dollars and twenty-four cents. After additional deductions for food purchases at the company store, the miner's net pay was only twenty cents! The meager net pay very likely was the incentive hungry miners in an earlier era had for working under a squeezing mine roof while continuously removing spalling coal pillars without stopping to drill, blast, or set props. By avoiding the effort and time required for drilling and blasting, they reduced the time and cost of so called "dead work". Not only were early miners unpaid for such work, but they were also back-charged for expenses related to drilling!

As work progressed at the Exeter mine, Hurricane Diane hit the Wyoming Valley, and the farmer near the mine called Dad that evening to say a stream of water was running into the mine entrance. Around midnight, Dad, Uncle Elmo, and I went to the mine, and with Uncle Elmo's dump-truck, we began dragging the mechanical loader, steam-shovel, and other equipment up the steep dirt road out of the pit. We did so as the hurricane raged and water streamed into the mine and pit from various directions. After pulling the equipment up the steep road out of the pit, the three of us rode the truck to Moosic to view other flood damage along the Lackawanna River. The next day after the storm, the pit appeared dry; but the Exeter mine was almost totally plugged with clay, sand, and silt, and had to be abandoned. Dad had been noticeably subdued when we toured storm damage along the Lackawanna River in the previous evening; but he never seemed deterred or discouraged when such serious setbacks occurred at his mines. When he drilled and loaded solid rock for weeks in the gangway at the Yatesville mine, without finding the main coal vein, is another example of such a setback. The major accidents to the drag-lines in Keystone and Old Forge are also examples of setbacks where a barrage of angry "PUTANNA CONCERTS" was certain; but Dad never exhibited any fear or despair. Many years later, during one of the countless stories we exchanged about the mines, my Father-in-Law, "Big Pete", recalled working underground in the general area of the Exeter mine. He explained how groundwater draining off the mountain on the west side of the valley was a major problem at his mine also. This is one example of the mundane topics ex-miners like he and I often re-hashed. The average person might respond, *"Whatever floats your boat;"* but again, many mining experiences can be not only unforgettable, but also inspiring.

In recent years, the farmland around the former Exeter Mine has been developed into residential housing, and as could be predicted, Dad's partially backfilled mine pit has been integrated into the development's storm water collection system. Years ago, before the development of water treatment plants, countless boreholes throughout The Wyoming Valley were drilled down into abandoned mines to discharge domestic and industrial wastes. Typically, throughout the Wyoming Valley, abandoned anthracite mines, whether intended or not, continue to serve as underground drainage routes for such wastes discharging down to the Susquehanna River. On recent trips back to The Wyoming Valley, I observed large volumes of orange, very contaminated water flowing out of abandoned mines and into the Susquehanna River. The contamination was clearly visible emanating from abandoned mines when I visited the site of the Knox Mine Disaster at the river's eastern bank, one-half mile downstream and south of Pittston. Another, much larger flow of bright orange contamination is visible slightly north of Pittston, at the confluence of the Susquehanna and Lackawanna Rivers near Old Forge. Viewing the "Google Earth" map in Figure 1, the huge flow of bright 'orange crud' can be seen contaminating the river at the upper left corner of that map. According to the internet, "The Old Forge Borehole" discharges forty million gallons of iron oxide into the Lackawanna River each day!

Acid Mine Drainage (AMD) is one of the on-going negative legacies of Anthracite Mining in the Wyoming Valley. Another negative is the damage caused by an occasional surface subsidence. In one example, a driver was stopped at a red light in Northeast Wilkes-Barre when his car dropped 6 or 8 feet into a sudden cave-in. After the driver crawled through a window and up to the road surface, the car suddenly disappeared into the abandoned mine below. When I was a structural engineer in Scranton, I recall designing some new building foundations and frameworks to resist collapse in the event of a cave-in. In some cases, the geotechnical engineer recommended silt or sand should be pumped through new boreholes to stabilize old mine chambers before constructing the new building foundations near the ground surface. For one multi-story apartment building, the geotechnical engineer oddly, but honorably, recommended in his final report that a sign should be hung on the wall inside the first floor hallway to alert occupants to the fact that an abandoned anthracite mine existed not far below the foundation. I often wondered if sleeping pills shouldn't also be stored near the sign to help relax the occupants each evening before going to bed.

Whether designing new structures or purchasing an existing structure, any available old mine maps for that location should first be reviewed to assess sub-surface risks. Cave-ins and contamination are not likely to cease in The Wyoming Valley in the current century.

CHAPTER X

THE YATESVILLE MINE (1956–57)

I was proud of my role in helping Dad start the mine in Yatesville (Bottom of Figure 1.) I even went along with Dad one evening when he visited the man who owned the lease rights to the coal to obtain the man's approval to start the mine. Mike Sarf, who lived in Yatesville, only one or two miles from the mine site, lay very ill in bed, and was the elderly owner of a large Coal Company. I can't recall the details of the conversation between Mike and Dad; but before we left, Mike mentioned his passion for accordion music. He also asked me to learn to play a classic John Phillip Sousa march that he himself used to play called, "Under the Double Eagle." About one week later, we returned with my accordion and at his request, I played Mike's favorite march five or six times. To this day I can still picture Mike lying in bed with a very huge grin, and his eyes swelling with tears as I played his favorite song. I regret not offering to perform it again for him in the weeks that followed.

Within days, Dad started the new mine but for whatever reason, Mike had either requested or encouraged Dad to install a mine hoist, tipple, and "gangway tunnel". After uncovering the vein with the bulldozer on the side of a hill, Dad and another miner, Bruno, began blasting the rock and coal, and hoisting it out to a new wood tipple that they constructed (See Figure 3). Following standard procedure, a ten or twelve foot long cut of coal was removed from the top half of the horizontal tunnel, and then a ten or twelve foot length of rock was blasted from the bottom half to deepen the tunnel and create the gangway. As mentioned previously, the typical gangway height needed to be tall enough to allow installation of railroad ties, steel rails, and a 4 or 5 foot high mine car. The top of the mine car had to be sufficiently below the bottom of the anthracite vein so that the coal could be easily scooped out of the vein and dumped into the top of the mine car. At a large colliery near Scranton, I once heard that rock cut from a gangway was dumped into a tipple from a mine car by use of a rugged piece of equipment nicknamed a "Mary Ann". Recently, I tried to find out where such an odd name originated for mine equipment. One historic account on the internet told me a mine owner named it after his mistress. Apparently, like boat owners named their yachts after their mistress, some miners named mine equipment in a similar way. It occurred to me that such nicknames for mining equipment weren't common knowledge in the anthracite coal fields, perhaps to avoid domestic disputes.

At Dad's new tipple in Yatesville, Uncle Elmo hauled coal and rock separately, as the coal and rock were sequentially blasted in the gangway tunnel. The coal in the gangway was poor quality and was temporarily stockpiled until it could be mixed with the good anthracite when the main vein was reached, and hopefully, very soon. Although the vein was only about three feet thick and extremely soft, Dad assumed it was the "vein outcrop" and guessed that continuing to extend the gangway would soon lead to the main vein and higher quality anthracite. Mine maps are typically vague in depicting locations of vein outcrops. Dad and Bruno struggled in the tunnel for several weeks while loading hard rock and low quality coal. They very likely observed, with envy, the prosperous coal tipple and mine operated by Mike's son 800 feet away, down in the flat valley where the vein was rich, thick and easily reached. Dad's new mine at a vein outcrop on the side of a hill was far more challenging.

For a few days, I worked as a "car topper" in the underground gangway with Dad and Bruno. As they shoveled the blasted rock into the mine car, I would also toss in small slabs and chunks of rock. As the loading reached the top of the car, I would line the four edges of the mine car with rock slabs to build a kind of 'retaining wall' that would enable them to shovel much more rock onto the top of the car. I built the walls as rapidly as they shoveled and recall Dad and Bruno smiling at each other without saying a word because with the aid of my rock 'retaining walls', the topping was climbing substantially higher than the top of the mine car's sideboards. Years later, my Father-in-Law, Big Pete, told me about a hardworking car topper who built up the sides so quickly, the exhausted and angry miners threw their shovels at the topper and yelled angrily, **"THE CAR IS FULL!"** In earlier years, miners were paid for each car loaded, and overly exuberant car toppers were not appreciated. At Dad's mines in Yatesville, men were paid the same daily rate of approximately eighteen dollars, regardless of quantity mined. Luckily, I was never hit with a shovel while topping mine cars!

Unfortunately, the gangway in the Yatesville Mine had progressed to a length of over one hundred feet; but the quality and thickness of the coal seam were not improving. This occurred because, unknowingly, we were not mining the true outcrop for the quality coal vein that was Dad's ultimate target. Such unforeseen mistakes in rough, rolling dog-holes weren't uncommon in coal veins that can't be accurately mapped. One day while searching the surrounding woods, Dad found the real outcrop in a wooded area about seven or eight hundred feet from the entrance to the initial gangway tunnel that had been incorrectly located. I could have kicked myself (**REAL HARD**)! I, too, had seen this outcrop at the ground surface, one day while I was tramping around the woods in prior weeks; but I neglected to bring it to Dad's attention! It was certainly my greatest personal disappointment of all my mining experiences. I could have received a big promotion and an increase in daily pay, perhaps from nine or ten dollars to eleven! Dad abandoned the initial gangway; but about fifty years later, I revisited this site. The tunnel was overgrown with trees and bushes and the deteriorated mine car was nearby, still serving as my personal, sentimental 'anthracite museum'. Unless one has had similar rich experience in their youth, it isn't likely they can understand the motivation for such nostalgic trips from Arizona back to The Wyoming Valley, and abandoned mine tunnels. Before leaving home on such trips, my wife typically admonishes me, "**DON'T ENTER THE MINE! DON'T GO IN!**" Fortunately, old mine entrances are typically backfilled, and only surface scars, rotted timbers, and a few relics are visible near the original site. Associates in my Phoenix office boost of family photos, signed baseballs, and golf trophies on their book shelves. With apologies to my wonderful family, the personal proud display on my office shelf is a square chunk of gleaming anthracite from the Yatesville mine.

After abandoning the gangway tunnel, Dad began to widen the newly found outcrop with the caterpillar bulldozer and excavate the storage pit for the steam-shovel. On occasion, Dad left the site in order to tend to his other dog-holes, and directed me to operate the dozer in his absence. I was probably only four or five years old when I first operated a bulldozer, that is, for three or four minutes while sitting on Dad's knee. As mentioned earlier, I enjoyed any opportunity to run the powerful machine. I think he was pleased with my proficiency with the machine that day in 1957 and told me so when he saw the volume of rock I had moved. Once the pit was dug, steam shovel and mechanical loader installed, the miners went to work and I continued my usual responsibilities of running the loader, dragging the coal out of the mine, and removing boney from Uncle Elmo's dump-truck. By this time, he and Dad had traded the old green Brockway for a powder blue 1954 F-900 Ford with the same eleven or twelve-ton capacity. Again, my Uncle painted the frame and wheel hubs a bright yellow. I'm certain Uncle Elmo drove the most artistic dump-trucks ever seen in The Wyoming Valley, with or without Marilyn Monroe calendars. The new 1954 Ford was much lighter than the 1947 Brockway, however, so that my Uncle no longer had to fear the State Police mobile truck scales, and the jail on Main Street in Dupont. Uncle Elmo's deteriorated F-900 dump-truck, now sixty-six years old, rests in a wooded gulley in another personal anthracite museum off the side of a two-lane paved road in Laflin.

Dad and Gino were now broadening their operations. They were operating dog-holes simultaneously in New Boston, Yatesville, and on Irish Hill. They also opened a coal reclamation process whereby small-sized anthracite, previously screened from mined coal and wasted near breakers, now became as valuable, or more so, than newly mined coal. With the advent of new household stoker furnaces after World War II, finely graded anthracite called "rice", "chestnut", "barley", and "buckwheat" were now in demand. The small-sized fine coal was also in great demand as fuel to generate electricity at large generating stations operated by power companies. The previously wasted fine coal was available in old abandoned stockpiles on the surface, easy to access, and only had to be screened and washed at the breaker. It could be found at the site of abandoned breakers, abandoned railroad beds, and landfills. Decades earlier, it had occasionally been re-installed by flushing it down thru boreholes back into abandoned mines to brace pillars and stabilize the surface. In the 1950's, my Father-in-Law, Pete, re-extracted this previously flushed coal from one of the three or four veins in his mine at the Diamond Colliery at the western end of Dorothy Street in West Scranton.

Dad also collected rent from the restaurant and home above it, after building Mother's dream ranch home on a hill behind the restaurant. The new home and restaurant were on the east side of State Route 315, one mile south of Dupont. The State eventually condemned and purchased these properties in 1962, in order to construct Interstate 81 with an access ramp that intersected Highway 315. The access ramp passes precisely at the previous location of the restaurant and hill-top home. Despite his growing success, Dad was still driven to take advantage of any small financial opportunity that presented itself. One day, a pile of old abandoned cast-iron parts and fittings lay strewn along a dismantled railroad track. After loading the pickup, we hauled the scrap metal to a local re-cycling shop where Dad probably received twenty or thirty dollars. A few days later, I also helped Dad load and recycle the steel "fishplates" that were about one foot square, one inch thick, and used to anchor steel railroad tracks to the wood cross-ties with thick steel spikes. This was the same rail track behind his Old Boston homestead where thirty to forty-five years earlier, Nonna often led her children to gather chunks of anthracite on the tops of large, slow-moving coal cars, and toss the chunks to the ground, below. This car-hopping practice to "purchase" fuel to heat homes during the frigid winter weather was quite common during the Great Depression. Evidence can still be seen in historical documentaries about The Wyoming Valley, where mothers and children are filmed running away from a slow moving train, and the incriminating eye of the on-board cameraman. Today we would refer to such activity as 'stealing' or 'theft'. During the Great Depression it was more sensitively referred to as "Boot-Legging". On another occasion on Irish Hill, the water company had long abandoned a buried twelve or sixteen-inch diameter cast iron pipeline. In quick succession starting at one exposed end, Dad used a heavy jack to force each pipe section up vertically out of the soil and to the ground surface, and then shattered each pipe section with a sledgehammer. I helped load the pieces of cast iron in the pickup, and we "boot-legged" them to the recycling yard. Recycling ventures like these were a holdover from Dad's difficult childhood and the economic hardships of the Great Depression. Certainly, Dad was not cold and hungry at this point, nor did he any longer need to hand-carry water out of the mine with two buckets. Nevertheless, like many miners in his generation, the after-effects of those very difficult years were embedded in him for his entire life. Quite often, Dad would use the money from recycled metals to throw an unscheduled picnic for the miners. On more than one occasion, the grimy group would emerge from the mine, sprawl on the ground, and enjoy a delicious feast of cheese, provolone, prosciutto, porquetta, or loansa, with hot green and red cherry peppers. When also placed on fresh home-made bread and accompanied by a cup of home-made red wine, the delicacy of the 'anthracite doghole picnic' was beyond anything available on current restaurant menus. During one such feast, the group of four or five coal-covered, exhausted miners sprawled out on the side of the railroad track near the mine in Yatesville. Eyeballing down the track with the other eye closed, they playfully argued through over-stuffed mouths whether the track was straight or crooked, as the freshly-made red wine flowed.

Camaraderie among the miners was unique. They partied, cried, and joked together. When it came to jokes, Dad's pranks often pushed his unfortunate target's limit of endurance. On one Friday or Saturday, he removed a dead dog from Highway 315 in front of the restaurant, took it to the mine, and placed it under the hood of one miner's car, while the miner was underground. When the miner returned to work on the following Monday morning, he complained to another unsuspecting miner that he had taken his family to Rocky Glen Amusement Park in Moosic on Sunday, and could not find the source of the foul odor in his car. The other, thoughtful miner inquired if the troubled miner had checked under the hood. At that point, I thought it best to turn and walk toward the shanty and could not hear what was transpiring because their voices behind me were drowned out by the loud noise from a nearby air compressor. Approaching the shanty, I turned and looked back at the miners to see that the car hood was wide open, they were standing about twenty-five feet away from the car, and waving their arms frantically as they argued. Around the same year, Dad bet another miner ten dollars that he could strike the headlight of the miner's old pickup with a rock from a distance of about thirty feet, and the miner accepted the bet. Dad underhanded a round rock, palm down like a bocce ball with which he was highly skilled, and shattered the headlight. In another case, when my sister, Carol, was in the tenth grade, a classmate of hers came courting at our door. Dad pretended to turn him away angrily at the front door, while waving the double barrel Fox shotgun. After the boy scurried away, Dad laughed uncontrollably. Of course, times are different today, and such pranks are likely to be viewed less humorously by authorities.

Invariably, everyone would break out in laughter after the prank; but Dad much more so than the victim. Once, while he was loading a dump-truck with the dragline, he hoisted a bucket of coal to the top of the truck and asked the driver to climb into the bucket to toss out a large slab of rock. While the trucker was inside the bucket, Dad lifted and held it about four feet above the truck. Dad turned and looked down at me from his seat in the dragline as tears of laughter rolled down his cheeks. I will never forget the look of terror on the driver's face, as he crouched down in the airborne bucket, and desperately clutched at its' sides. After Dad set the bucket back down on the truck, the driver jumped off the top of the truck, dumped the truckload of coal on the ground, and drove away.

Through the years, I had heard of similar pranks pulled long ago by his father, and thus, I believe Dad either inherited the gene from Nonno, or copied it through admiration for his Father, as I did for mine. However, based on the following, Nonno's pranks may have been even more questionable than Dad's. Adjacent to their back-yard chicken coup, Nonno and Nonna also had a few pigs and goats. Apparently, it wasn't uncommon to feed pigs cooked worms in order to flush existing live crawlers from the pig's stomach with the cooked ones. One day, a young, uneducated miner asked Nonno if that was 'tasty spaghetti' Nonno was cooking on the coal stove. It happened to be near dinner time, and so I think you know how Nonno 'courteously and hospitably' treated the unsuspecting miner. I'll end the story there. (**UGH!**) I have concluded that Nonno's pranks, while both extreme and humorously intended, were rooted in the same stern demeanor that was so critical to his survival underground. I also suspect that crude style of demeanor was also necessary to his family's successful subsistence during an historic period of severe economic hardship. Yes, I know there were many Grandfathers who very thoughtfully provided for their families without such crude demeanor during The Great Depression; but it's my "Nonno Excuse", and I am sticking with it.

They say, "Apples don't fall far from the tree," as if I could have been so lucky; but now that I think of it, I too pursued the "prank gene". In fact, I may have even surpassed Dad and Nonno on at least one or two occasions. When I was a senior in high school, my six-year-old sister and I were home alone late one evening when Linda bolted out of her dark bedroom, ran into the TV room where I was sitting, and tearfully shuttered, "*SOMETHING IS TAPPING ON MY WINDOW!*" I replied, "*Don't cry. It's just Nunzio.*" Nunzio Massarra Jr. was my good friend in high school. In the dark bedroom, I cranked the window open, poked the 12-gage double barrel into the evening darkness, blasted both barrels toward the woods, and then in mock anger yelled, "**WHO'S OUT THERE?**" No, I wasn't crazy. I was sixteen. Nunzio later reported the gun barrel was only a short distance above his head, and in the darkness, the flame out of the end of the barrel was two feet long. In recent years I'm asked, "*WOW! How did you know you wouldn't blast his head off?*" I replied, "*That's easy. I used to mow the lawn in that area every weekend. Therefore, I knew the window was at least six feet and six inches above ground, and Nunzio is only six feet and three inches tall!* Following another evening of fun and frolic in the twelfth grade, I apologetically announced to classmates Nunzio and Tom that I "could not" stop in front of their houses in Inkerman (bottom left corner of Fig. 1); but instead, they would need to hastily jump from my 1952 Plymouth as it coasted along in second gear. The sight of Nunzio frantically trying to avoid crashing into trees, as he dashed through the woods in a desperate effort to catch up to his momentum, is forever etched in my memory. Obviously, these pranks were far too dangerous, and I am happy to report that (most of) my pranks in recent years have attained a much higher level of maturity. More importantly, Nunzio and Tom are still good friends, and because of my very thoughtful coaching, both became more athletic. Furthermore, Nunzio also learned how to use doorbells. All dangerous and immature pranks aside, there isn't any legal favor I wouldn't do for my life-long friends, Tom Ruskey of Inkerman, and Nunzio Massara Jr. of Mechanicsburg, Pennsylvania.

Tossing each other's cap in the air and shooting at them with their rifles, wrestling on the ground, and other playful games, were also common among the miners. They called one unusual game "chiqueta." Each miner would take a bocce ball and throw it underhanded as far as they could along Old Boston Road, which forms a horseshoe about two miles in total length, to see whose toss would roll furthest. The road was not paved as it is now, but probably held the national record at that time for number and size of potholes per foot of road. Thus, the challenge was to clear obstructions and chose the best route to heave the bocce. The game would proceed from one end of the mining settlement to the other, and return back to the Old Boston Club House near the south end of the horseshoe. The miner with the fewest winning throws when they returned to the clubhouse had to buy the beer. Hard labor, vendettas, games, humor, **and** pranks, were all part of a miner's lifestyle. All of this behavior is also colorfully portrayed in the movie, "The Molly Maguires", except "pranks" are replaced by acts of "mine sabotage".

CHAPTER XI

TRUCKS, DOZERS, AND A
TREACHEROUS MINE (1958)

I continued to operate the mechanical loader and pitch rock/boney off the coal trucks at the Yatesville mine during the summer, school vacations, and on weekends. At Irish Hill, I also helped Dad start another mine there, while the Yatesville mine continued in operation. At Irish Hill we built a sloping wood ramp from the entrance of the mine up to a point where the truck could be loaded directly by the scoop of the mechanical loader, so that another steam-shovel was not necessary. As usual, Dad's creativity in solving mining problems was remarkable. He didn't deliberate, plan, sketch, or request a carpenter's assistance. He built tunnels, tipples, ramps, shanties, loader buckets, as if naturally driven. Bruno was the foreman for the new Irish Hill mine, and Dad paid him for each truckload of coal. He was a lifelong friend, and I even named my hunting dog "Bruno", instead of "Tom", or "Nunzio". Friendship aside, Bruno became annoyed with me whenever I overloaded the truck. Nevertheless, I knew how my 'bread was buttered', and I routinely "over-topped" the coal truck with the mechanical loader. Since the coal up high in the Valley was a lower quality, Dad had it trucked approximately two or three miles to the west and mixed with the higher quality anthracite down at the New Boston mine. After mixing, it would benefit from the higher price received for the New Boston coal. The haul was over an ungraded 'pioneer trail' at about five or ten miles per hour, curving around and over hills, and adjacent to the edges of numerous abandoned, deep strip mines.

After I loaded (heaped) the final truckload one day with the mechanical loader, I was anxious to get behind the wheel of the Ford F-900 dump truck, and negotiate the rugged pioneer trail. I tried to persuade Bruno to let me haul the load to New Boston. Very reluctantly, but perhaps happy to go home sooner, Bruno relented. Approximately half-way down the rocky pioneer road during the unforgettable haul, I encountered a deep drainage swale in the trail, which I knew would tip the top-heavy truck precariously, no matter how slowly I negotiated it. At the last second, I elected to instead steer down a parallel, unused trail that was generally flat, but muddy. The truck bogged down, was axle deep in the mud, and wheels spun without moving forward. This would certainly have been an appropriate time for a "putanna concert"; but fortunately for co-workers in my engineering office, I never picked up on that part of Dad's boot camp training. A cell phone also would have been helpful; but they didn't exist at that time, and I'm probably the only guy around who STILL doesn't own one today! I kneeled down in the mud and began scooping it away from the truck's tires and axle with my arms. After about sixty minutes of crawling in and clearing away the muck, I saw Dad speeding and bouncing up the pioneer trail in his brand-new, black 1958 Lincoln. He had showered, dressed, and apparently was headed for the Old Boston Clubhouse before he called Bruno to find out why I had not yet returned home. From a distance beyond the quagmire, he sounded more upset than relieved; but from the way he sped up the pioneer trail with the Lincoln, I suspect the opposite was true. He yelled that he was going for the bulldozer and slowly drove away. I continued to pull the mud from around the tires and axle with my arms, and drove the truck out of the marsh just as Bruno arrived. Neither Dad nor Bruno ever said anything more about the event; but personally, I thought I demonstrated some pretty good "trucking and mucking" skills. Although my family doesn't agree, I may have also demonstrated the exaggerated importance that they currently place on cell phones! I'll likely continue to regard the device as a nuisance, until I become desperately stranded somewhere.

On another day, Bruno had driven Dad's pickup to the mine in Irish Hill, and at the end of the work day, I again coaxed Bruno to let me drive it home. He reluctantly sat on the rider's side as I excitedly drove along the dirt road from Irish Hill, and then down Suscon Road. A fresh snow had fallen and the paved road leading three miles west from Suscon to Dupont was icy. About 2-1/2 miles east of Dupont, the pavement descends a very steep hill for about 1/4 of a mile. Near the bottom of the hill, two or three vehicles were stuck in the snow and drivers were standing near their stalled vehicles. As we descended the icy hill, the pickup began sliding and gyrating from side to side, and I had only partial control. For some strange reason that I still do not fully understand, I laughed uncontrollably as the pickup slid faster, sideways, and dangerously between the stalled vehicles, barely clearing them on either side. Granted, it sounds crazy; but I wasn't. Again, I was sixteen! Bruno swore later that one of the stranded drivers peed his pants as we skidded and swirled past. It was another one of those occasions when I like to think that my trucking skills bailed me out again; but perhaps 'shear luck' played a more important part. Nevertheless, Dad may have been impressed by my driving skills and/ or my enthusiasm to drive coal trucks. One day shortly after receiving my driver's license at age 16, Dad allowed me to haul coal from the mine in Yatesville to the Breaker in Hughestown (Top of Figure I). I made seven exciting hauls that day with a Ford F-900 dump truck and blasted the air horn each time I passed Uncle Elmo going in the opposite direction in his F-900.

The mine in Yatesville (Bottom of Figure 1) was positioned on top of a steep hillside where an existing railroad (still) runs along the base of the tall hill. The coal had been strip-mined many years earlier in the flat valley beyond the railroad tracks; but, of course, the open pit strip mine had to stop well clear of the rail tracks. Dad's dog-hole tunnel sloped steeply down the hillside for about 200 feet, and then the tunnel turned ninety degrees to the left to run level along the base of the hill and under the railroad. The dog-hole tunnel layout had great advantages and disadvantages. The advantage was that after the main tunnel was advanced down the sloping hillside, and then turned left to run along the base of the hill, side chambers could then be blasted back up the steep hill. Thus, in the side slope chambers, each blasted cut of coal naturally slid down the steep side slope to the main tunnel at the bottom of the hill, thereby reducing the scoop's travel distance. Sheet metal was anchored between the props on the side slope so that almost each entire cut of coal slid down to the flat area of the mine, and piled there in the main tunnel at the base of the hill. Thus, hand shovels were hardly ever required. The loader could easily and quickly scoop it from the pile along the base of the hill, pull the scoop back through the main tunnel, and drag the coal up the hill and out to the steam-shovel. However, there was another major, unsafe drawback reported by the miners. Like an imminent catastrophe, the mine rumbled and shook dramatically each time a train passed approximately twenty-five or thirty feet overhead, thereby threatening a roof collapse.

Despite the difficult conditions, Dad decided to open a second dog-hole, on the same hilltop, about six or seven hundred feet from the first dog-hole, in order to continue mining the coal along the steep hillside, and under the railroad at the base of the hill. After starting the new excavation, Dad directed me to continue removing the soft overburden with the bulldozer to form the new pit. Each day, after running the mechanical loader at the first dog-hole, I would operate the bulldozer at the new second site, while Dad and the other miners drilled the next cut of coal and set props in the existing dog-hole. When he emerged from the mine at the end of each day, I recall how pleased he was with the progress I was making in excavating the new pit for the second, nearby dog-hole.

The entrance to the new dog-hole tunnel slanted from right to left as shown in Figure 12; but after progressing forty or fifty feet, the vein also began sloping steeply down the hill toward the railroad. The twisting and turning are truly impossible to accurately diagram in Figure 12. Miners traveled through the four and one/half foot tall mine by crawling and sliding from prop to prop. Although it was easier to walk along the bottom of the side-slope at the vein's left sidewall shown in the diagram, or coal "rib" as miners termed it, this was the dangerous un-propped zone, and the necessary, unobstructed travel path for the scoop. About seventy-five feet from the entrance, the vein's floor and roof suddenly pinched together and the vein of anthracite terminated at what miners call a "roll" in the vein. Dad and Gino instinctively knew the vein must resume nearby because they could see where the same vein had been strip-mined years earlier in the flat area, down beyond the railroad track. They continued drilling and blasting through the rock for a few days and finally found where the vein resumed again beyond the 'roll'. Now, however, the vein and tunnel continued to slope downward, but due to the roll, the tunnel twisted and turned until it reached the flatland under the railroad.

In addition to mine vibrations and twisting slopes, breathing in the undulating mine was difficult until side chambers could be mined back up the side-slope to daylight at the vein's surface outcrop at the top of the hill. A safety lamp hung from a prop and a small flame flickered inside the glass lamp to tell the miners that there was still enough oxygen where they were working. If the flame died away, it was the signal to evacuate quickly because carbon dioxide was filling the chamber. The miners referred to this condition as "black damp," which through the years, asphyxiated countless anthracite miners. In this and the previous chapter, I described the pride I took at that time in my role in helping Dad start the mine in Yatesville. However, in later years that followed, it dawned on me that this treacherous mine is a common example of the many dog-holes that never should have been started. The mine was very productive; but extremely twisting, sloping, vibrating under the railroad, and treacherous. Thankfully, Dad never asked me to enter this treacherous mine. I even feel uncomfortable today just writing about it. However, state and federal mine inspectors apparently didn't seem to have any problem with it, as long as it was propped. In 2019 I toured Guadalcanal in the Solomon Islands with a World War II Historical Tour company. The jungle battles of John Basilone, Mitchell Paige, Al Schmidt and other Guadalcanal medalists, were more perilous than the miners' battles in the treacherous Yatesville dog-hole. Nevertheless, comparisons can be made to demonstrate how the risks to the survival of very heroic men were similar at both 'battle sites'.

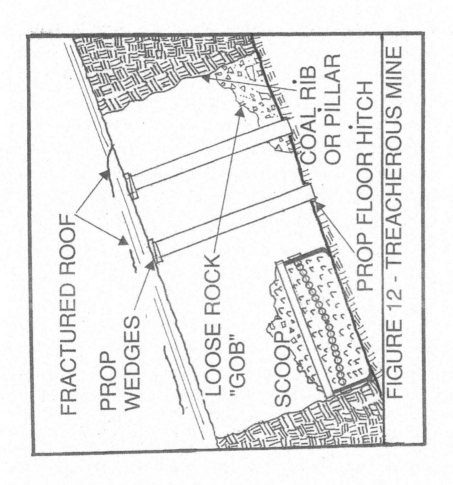

FRACTURED ROOF

PROP WEDGES

LOOSE ROCK "GOB"

SCOOP

COAL RIB OR PILLAR

PROP FLOOR HITCH

FIGURE 12 – TREACHEROUS MINE

Even in the midst of their daily perils, the miners seldom lost their sense of humor and love for pranks. On one occasion, the quality of the air in the mine, though adequate to keep the tiny flame in the safety lamp burning, was marginal and making it difficult to breathe. They instructed one young, uneducated miner to grab a bunch of the small paper "tamping bags" used to plug dynamite drill holes. They requested the young man go out and fill each small tamping bag with air at the entrance to the mine, and empty the air from the bags back at the face of the mine where the men were working. The miners laughed for days after the inexperienced, but hard-working young man, fell for the prank. They occasionally asked him to sing for them also, which he enthusiastically enjoyed doing. *"Cruising Down the River on a Sunday Afternoon"*, sang out hilariously as, *"Toos-ing Down the River...."* in a non-musical monotone, and the humor helped the miners endure the very treacherous working conditions.

At the end of one shift, however, Gino Popple crawled out of the mine in quiet, but obvious frustration. Upon standing erect, he threw one glove ten feet into the air and then the other, likewise. When conditions in a mine were very tough, Gino would often say with well-deserved pride in his emotional strength and physical endurance, *"I bulled my way through it."* On this day, however, he continued to trudge toward his pickup without saying a word to me. He did not want to make a living at this mine, and for good reason. Even a mythological 'minotaur' would struggle to "bull his way" through a day in this treacherous dog-hole! To add to his dilemma, Gino's right hand was crippled since birth, and it prevented him from gripping a shovel and other tools properly and firmly. Instead of firmly gripping the shovel with a hand near each end, he would lift the heavy end with the handle supported on his right wrist. Twenty-five years later, however, he would own coal collieries, outdoor theaters, a hotel, and confide to me that his financial accounts were worth "thirteen big ones." As he put it, a "big one" was his slang expression for "one million dollars."

I can easily recall the brute strength and passion of the men who worked that mine, besides Dad and Gino. One can easily imagine that only the very strong ones stuck around. Ernie Renfer worked his own small dairy farm in Suscon each evening after his shift at the mine. Ernie and his wife, Erna, raised their family on that farm in a quaint little valley at the end of Chapel Road. He was packed with muscle after a lifetime of simultaneous hard labor in the mines and on his dairy farm. Dad said Ernie often snapped shovels after shoving them under and lifting large chunks of coal or rock. Even during normal conversation, Ernie's deep, reverberating voice resonated volume and power in an unusual way. Dad also joked that when they were hunting, and Ernie was booming his thundering yells through the woods to flush out deer, the emerging, frantic deer were happy to be shot! When telling me a story with his resounding, deep voice, Ernie would look close into my face and, with one eye closed like a pirate, emphasize his point by waving his right forefinger in my face, and periodically, rap his knuckles hard on my chest with the back of his same right hand as he spoke. As if he had to impress me any further, he emerged from the mine after one day of hard work and, in coal-crusted boots, clothes, helmet, and headlamp, did five push-ups at age forty-one or forty-two with one arm bent behind his back. Ernie's strength resulted from years of hard labor, and not work-outs at a gym. When we visited him one evening while he was seated on a stool in his barn and milking a cow, he asked me to turn in the other direction so as to, in his words, "check something out", in the corner of his barn. After I turned in that direction, Ernie then nailed the back of my neck with a powerful gush from one of the cow's utters. For days after his prank, no amount of scrubbing removed the raw milk's very strange odor from my neck.

Bruno Panattieri was another big, strong miner who liked to recount stories about his record of '9 and 1' as an amateur heavyweight boxer in the United States Navy during World War II. He and his wife, Anna, raised their family in the small anthracite mining village of Keystone, which is one mile north of Wilkes-Barre. He would lift his chin and pointing to his left nostril, display the bent septum received in his tenth bout. Bruno worked very hard, and when he once overslept, I rode with Dad to Bruno's home, where Dad knocked on his door to wake him. This kind of tolerance was just one small example of Dad's friendship with the miners. Victor Augustini was another broad-shouldered, hardworking miner with brute strength. He and his wife, Della, raised their family in the small mining village of Sebastapool, which adjoins the southern boundary of the City of Pittston. Our families occasionally enjoyed a cookout together at Lake Wallenpaupak east of Scranton, or Nay Aug Park in Scranton, where Victor was usually the recognized expert at roasting chickens on an open fire. Miners seemed to enjoy working with Dad and stuck with him for years. Some told me, however, they had never been pushed so hard. I am convinced they could tolerate it because although he pushed constantly, he did so respectfully and worked even harder alongside of them. He was also their good friend with a great sense of humor. Years later, I decided that Dad's was the ideal style of supervision, leadership, and executive management, minus the pranks.

That summer, I had another very memorable experience of a very different kind. I was practicing my accordion in the study room in the basement of our home, when the daughter of my parents' very close friends made a social visit. She came with her girlfriend, and as I played a classic tune from the 1940s called, *"In The Mood,"* the two very attractive eighteen-year-olds, who had just graduated from Pittston High School in 1958, jitterbugged to the music. They very likely were the precise model ABBA related to in their 1976 hit song, "*Dancing Queen(s)*". However, their impact on me can be more precisely interpreted by the Bee Gees hit of 1977 titled, "*Saturday Night Fever*". Suddenly, it dawned on me that just like draglines, bulldozers, and big green Brockway dump-trucks, pretty girls also had an equally-deserved place in this world. I hardly spoke to girls at school and recall going to only one high school dance, at which I likely didn't even dance. After the 'jitterbug in the basement', however, I began to view pretty girls in a different "mood". As they say, "*Better late than never!*"

Nevertheless, the pretty girl's parents, Sam and Doris Sperrazza, frightened the heck out of me one evening when I overheard them tell my parents that during our upcoming joint family vacation in Atlantic City, their daughter and I could go our own way at the shore while the two families vacationed. I was "in the mood" alright, but fearfully unable to manage it. A day or two before the scheduled trip, I strongly insisted to my parents that I was not interested in Atlantic City and wanted to stay behind with Nonna where "I could make better use of my time." I probably spent my valuable time watching reruns of "*Cheyenne*" or "*Ramar of the Jungle*" on TV, or in some equally "valuable" pastime. In retrospect, my meager, undeveloped skills in social communication had probably been caved in, squashed, or trucked away by my significant bulldozing and trucking skills. I'm not a psychologist, but perhaps this social deficiency may have been the single, negative effect resulting from my extended training in Anthracite Boot Camp. Fortunately, the negative effect totally dissipated over the next few years after 1959, I hope.

CHAPTER XII

BOOT CAMP GRADUATION (1959)

The year began to unfold, continue, and end with a series of very sad events, including the Knox Mine Disaster. The Susquehanna River broke into the Knox Mine in Port Griffith (Left edge of Figure 1) just south of Pittston on January 22. Eighty-one miners were trapped, and twelve of them were forever entombed. Amazingly, it was later reported that roofs of some mine chambers existed within only six or seven feet beneath the bed of the very large river! I personally knew one of the deceased miners. He was a kind gentleman by the name of Frank Burns, who occasionally had inspected Dad's mine on behalf of the coal company that owned the rights to the coal. Uncle Jim Musto escaped up one of the gangways just ahead of the rising water. Dad's cousin, Pacifico (Joe) Stella, survived and received an award for leading a group of trapped miners to a small, remote, abandoned opening that once was called The Eagle Air Shaft. Amadeo Pancotti received a medal for clawing his way up the clogged, abandoned air shaft to get help and lower a rope to rescue 32 other miners. It took several days for authorities to plug the gaping hole that was about thirty feet square in the river bottom. I will forever picture the huge railroad boxcars being dumped into the gaping hole to plug the whirlpool into the mine. Even today, video of the giant steel boxcars whirling down into the mine can be readily viewed on the internet. The whirlpool sucked down more than fifty such monster coal cars; but by then, submerged veins from Scranton to Wilkes-Barre had to be permanently abandoned because of the prohibitive cost of pumping the ten billion gallons of flood water. Later in the year, the very sad tragedy of the Knox event was repeated for our family when our very close friend, Victor Augustini, was killed in a roof collapse at Dad's mine in New Boston. Victor left behind his wonderful wife, Della, young son, and daughter.

Although I had been a successful student for three years at West Pittston High School, where my parents were paying my tuition so I could academically prepare for college and medical school, my grades suddenly deteriorated during the initial semester of my senior year. In my new-found "Mood", school had become quite boring; but as the years passed, I became suspicious that my under-developed social skills may have also contributed to the academic problem. Dad was forced to transfer me to Jenkins Township High School in Inkerman to graduate. After high school graduation, our congressman declined my request for an appointment to the U.S. Naval Academy, but instead, granted an appointment to the U.S. Merchant Marine Academy. I told my parents that I did not want to be a doctor, as they requested, nor did I want to be a merchant ship officer. Instead, I wanted to join the United States Marines. My parents were disappointed; but in recent years, it gradually dawned on me that Dad's training, and Mother's training in 'Honor' as mentioned in this book's Dedication, were instrumental in leading me toward the military and The Corps. I asked the marine recruiter to speak to Dad in an effort to obtain Dad's approval for me to enlist. The sergeant explained very diplomatically to Dad, *"If he doesn't want to go to college now, he may feel differently after his four years of service. Besides, his test scores were very good and he qualifies for advanced technical training."* Dad relented and signed his approval.

Looking back at all the disappointment I created, I am amazed that I was able to obtain approval for my request from such a demanding Father. Thus, Dad discharged me from Anthracite Boot Camp, and transferred me to U.S. Marine Corps Boot Camp.

My parents were very unhappy with my request; but it was not long before Dad again displayed his unfaltering support. My new classmates at Jenkins Township High School soon learned of my parents' summer cottage on the Lehigh River at Thornhurst in The Pocono Mountains. They requested that I ask Dad to allow us to have our graduation party there. Mother was leery, but Dad said, "*It's o.k. They just want to have a little fun and some beer*," and Dad added emphatically, "**BUT NO GIRLS!**" The night of the party, one of the five or six girls there said, "*Your dad just pulled up out front and wants to talk to you.*" Suddenly, I felt I was again under the screaming dragline climbing up the steep hill; but this time, it also felt as if the dragline's crawler brakes weren't working. When I went outside the cottage, Bruno was behind the wheel, and Dad cranked the window down on the rider's side. Very sternly, he said, "*I thought I told you no girls!*" I looked down at the ground without saying anything, and after a few very uncomfortable seconds, Dad said, grinning, "*Go get us 2 bottles of beer.*" In a few minutes more, he and Bruno drove off. He probably knew I didn't have the courage to tell my new high-school friends that they couldn't bring their girlfriends. I also suspect that he (very accurately) observed, "This is a good group of kids having clean fun," or perhaps he circled back later to double check. Years later, I vowed that I would be as supportive and lenient with my own teenagers as Dad and Mother were with me. My vow was subsequently tested numerous times in the years that followed. As an example, one son returned to Arizona without my car after a trip to California where the car was impounded for illegal parking. On another occasion I landed at JFK International in New

York, and discovered my credit card was missing from my wallet when I walked up to the car rental desk. Around the same time, my other son sneaked off with my car, and bumped our house when returning back into our garage. Also, after I purchased a red sports car for my beautiful daughter when she turned sixteen, her only response was, "*It has potential.*" In my opinion, I passed, with flying colors, all the tests of my vow to support my children in the same manner Dad and Mother supported me. I also can report, today, that my three children would make any parent quite proud of their achievements!

The photo on the next page with my hand on Dad's shoulder was taken at my going-away party in July of 1959. On the next day, my parents took me to the train station in Wilkes - Barre for the long trip to Marine Corps Boot Camp at Parris Island, South Carolina. The recruiter elected to publicize my enlistment, including a picture in the newspaper with Dad and I shaking hands before I boarded the train. In the newspaper photo, it appears obvious Dad is trying hard to smile. On the next day, as several other recruits and I stepped down from the train's steps in Yemesee, South Carolina, I will forever recall the view of the arm-waving, cursing marine drill instructor charging from the railroad station to "greet" us. My first day of Marine Corps Boot Camp reminded me of the huge mine collapse on my first day of Anthracite Boot Camp in Chapter V.

During my second or third week of boot camp, Dad wrote a letter in which he told me about the latest events at home. Just as when we shook hands before I boarded the train for Boot Camp, his words were warm without a hint of emotional sentiment. Anthracite miners did not openly communicate emotion, at least not Dad. Besides, I was confident in our feelings toward each other, and spoken words were not necessary, nor mean anything more. At the end of his letter, he asked me if it was okay to invest the $3,500 that I had accumulated in our joint bankbook during the years he had paid me for my work at the mines. He wrote that he thought investing it in stock market blue chips would be a good idea. What I would pay today for a copy of that letter! It was the only time Dad ever asked me for my approval to do anything. Perhaps in a state of shock, I wrote back what might be interpreted as a touch of sarcasm that I regret to this day when I said, "*Yes, it's okay with me. Besides, I always regarded the money as more yours than mine.*" That certainly was a foolish statement on my part, because there was absolutely no way Dad would ever take any of the money for his personal use. I also think that what I really meant was to respectfully propose that, "*What's mine is yours.*" The stocks that he purchased under our joint names were the bluest of blue chips - American Telephone and Telegraph, Continental Can, and Keystone Custodian Stock Fund. Thus, my seven and one-half years of part-time labor at the anthracite dog-holes continued to pay handsome financial dividends.

On September 10, 1959, I was in a prone position firing my M-1 rifle at targets on the rifle range on Parris Island. Between shots, I periodically glanced out of the corner of my eye toward my drill instructor approximately 100 yards away, as he approached from across a broad, open field. He was walking slowly with his head down. His demeanor was remarkably different from his running, growling, cursing, hand-waving style I had witnessed over the prior six or seven weeks. I sensed something wasn't right. He shuffled up to me and said, "**Let's go. Your mother wants you home.**" Marine recruits don't question drill sergeants, and without further explanation, the sergeant took me to the supply warehouse for a dress uniform, and to the train depot in the nearby town of Yemesee. Although I had to make two or three train changes along the way, I never called home. Besides, I knew exactly what had happened the instant the drill instructor said, "*Your mother wants you home*"; but I did not want to hear it. The next evening, as I got out of the taxi a few hundred feet from our house on the hill, two friends working at a nearby service station, walked over to the taxi and solemnly said to me, "**We're sorry. He was a great man**," thereby confirming my fearful anticipation of an accident at the Yatesville mine. Our home was filled with family and friends, and since I had not eaten for some time, I rode with Uncle Nick Vigilante to a curb-service diner on South Main Street, Pittston. There, we ate sandwiches and cried together in his car. It was, and remains, the saddest day of my life. As odd as it may seem, whenever I hear the uniquely styled, gentle and solemn music of "The Lonely Shepherd", by James Last and Gheorghe Zamfir, it brings to mind that extremely sad period of time in 1959.

Even with the benefit of hindsight, it is perplexing to see how Dad's plight, and that of more than 100,000 other anthracite miners, escaped them and their families before the inevitable occurred:

explosions, dangerous equipment, cave-ins, black damp, black lung, flooding. Why be a miner, and why didn't families do more to get their sons, fathers, or husbands out of that "Catastrophe Waiting to Happen"? Despite his mean reputation, Nonno sincerely tried, and successfully kept his sons out of the mines while he was alive. If Dad had obeyed his deceased father's order, Dad might have survived an additional 40 or 50 years. For these very courageous men, the reason meaningful action wasn't taken by their families may be embedded in Chapters 2 and 3. Another reason may be embedded in my Mother's words to me many years ago. Mother once told me that she never once doubted Dad's intelligence and judgement. He always seemed indestructible. In addition to the tragic loss of Dad, Victor, and Frank Burns, I sadly witnessed two other friends, Tucci and Nunzio's father, desperately trying very hard to breathe while in the final throes of Black Lung Disease. Although he died when I was only nine or ten, I still remember the large blue scar that Aunt Vienna's husband, Uncle Primo Carnevale, carried on the side of his forehead after a mine explosion.

The following is a list of the accidents, physical problems, and near misses that Dad endured from 1942 to 1959. The sad list is even more striking when one realizes these are only the incidents that I witnessed or heard about. The complete list, if known, would likely be twice as long:

1942: A dump truck that he was driving at a mine on a steep hill in Mocanaqua lost its brakes and he jumped clear as it ran away.

1943: Received a broken leg in a mine accident and was on crutches for an extended period.

1948: Running a bulldozer on top of a hill behind Old Boston and jumped clear just as the dozer jumped out of gear and plunged into a deep strip mine.

1949: Accidentally swallowed fuel oil while siphoning from a fuel drum and became very ill.

1954: Fractured wrist between top of scoop and roof of mine when the scoop suddenly shifted.

1954: After pushing the plunger, a boulder blasted out of the strip mine, bounced under the truck that he assumed was shielding him, and struck his knee to cause severe swelling.

1954: Received bad burns on his hands in the mine after gripping power lines for which the power had supposedly been turned off.

1955: Operated a dragline with the boom passing repeatedly under a high voltage power line. The boom of the dragline suddenly lurched and bumped the high voltage line, but he apparently was electrically grounded and unaffected by the large voltage that passed through him.

1955: Struggled to free a dragline from the mud and nearly tipped it into the stripping hole.

1957: Was prospecting for a coal mining opportunity in an abandoned mine in Old Forge. Encountered very bad air and barely made it back up the steep slope to fresh air.

1958: While running the bulldozer in a frigid blizzard, the steel cable that hoists the blade jammed in a pulley. He lost the tip of a finger when he suddenly freed the cable with his hands.

1958: Probably from excessive coal dust, had problem breathing freely, and a doctor had to chip away bone in a sinus or nostril passageway with a mallet and small medical chisel.

1959: Killed under the collapse of a mine roof on September 9 in Yatesville.

EPILOGUE

ANTHRACITE BOOT CAMP LESSONS LEARNED

To sell a few hundred copies of "ANTHRACITE BOOT CAMP" would be wonderful; but that wasn't the primary objective of this non-fiction novel. The main objective was to help define for family members, the descendants of anthracite miners, and for the descendants of other early settlers in The Wyoming Valley, the heritage and lessons passed on to us by our ancestors. In retrospect, Anthracite Boot Camp enabled me to witness and receive inspirational training that revolved around five basic courses that can improve the quality of anyone's life: (1) Honor, (2) Focused Diligence, (3) Leadership, (4) Collaboration, (5) Diplomacy. Obviously, one doesn't need to attend Anthracite Boot Camp to learn and apply the courses. In my particular case, Boot Camp made me aware of the existence and value of the courses. Although the final grades that I personally achieved in each course may(will) be debated by friends and co-workers, the high importance of these subjects should be obvious to all who have been around fifty or sixty years to witness the weakening that has occurred in our nation's solidarity.

(1) SENSE OF HONOR

I feel this is the inspiration of first and foremost importance. It goes without saying that one can achieve the inspiration in a variety of different ways and experiences. As mentioned in the book's "Dedication", my initial personal training in "HONOR" began when I was a young boy maturing under the guidance of my Mother. She never mentioned the word 'honor', but time after time, whenever she saw anyone treat something or someone dishonorably, her emphatic response was always the same three words: "**THAT'S NOT RIGHT**"! Mother's Father, Nicholo, set the ultimate example for me. As a masonry contractor in the Pittston area, he once built a large masonry block wall that he subsequently felt wasn't his best work. Even though his client was quite satisfied with it, Grandfather Nicholo said, "**IT'S NOT RIGHT!**" He then tore down and re-built the large wall at his own expense! I don't know what the problem was with the wall; but neither did the client. This is a classic example of the ultimate level of customer service that stems from a personal Sense of Honor. In contrast, today, many service providers often focus on opportunities to cut corners and shave costs, even if it differs from their contract agreement. It seems odd to me that one hardly ever hears the word "Honor" mentioned in our society.

For the Anthracite Mining Industry, this Sense of Honor is rooted in the hard work, pain, perseverance, and pride demonstrated in the Industry over a period of one hundred and seventy years. My wife of fifty-seven years, Frances, has been an outstanding partner, and a wonderful mother to our three children. Only in recent years has it dawned on me that her own family's direct connection to anthracite mining had been more than just a subtle attraction to me. Again, one might conclude that my sense of values had been misplaced; but not if they fully understood my references to the roots of 'honor' that I cite. Whenever her parents would visit us in Arizona from their home in Exeter, Pennsylvania, her Dad and I would remain at the kitchen table for hours after dinner and talk about the mines after Frances and her mother, Dora, retired to the TV room. Her Dad and I thoroughly enjoyed exchanging experiences and stories about anthracite mining in The Wyoming Valley. Big Pete had five proud stories for each of mine. Recently, I met another engineer who had similar youthful experience in the coal mines of West Virginia. After he related his experience, his wife mentioned the sense of honor and pride her husband demonstrated whenever he recounted such stories about his coal mining ancestors. Unless one has actually lived similar experiences, it may not be possible to fully grasp and comprehend the inner strength and inspiration that such experience can bestow whenever the origin of that inspiration is re-called or re-visited. An opportunity to sense this may be detected if one visits the Anthracite Coal Museum in Scranton, or The Eckley Miners Village near Hazleton, as I have done on several occasions. In my case, the history of the U.S. Marine Corps also contributed, as exemplified in the classic Hollywood Movie, "A FEW GOOD MEN". Another opportunity to grasp the true meaning of 'honor' may be to join a guided tour of Marine Corps World War II monuments in the Solomon Islands, as I did in 2019 on Guadalcanal and Tulagi. For me and others inspired by such experiences, these aren't just leisurely pastimes or vacation "Get-A-Ways".

It is possible that if I had spent my entire professional life as a coal miner, or if I served as a Marine in Viet Nam, I might feel differently, today, about 'honor'. Nevertheless, I do know that my experience makes me wish I had accomplished more to serve my Country and the Corps. Regardless, as it turned out, my Mother's guidance and my youthful training in Anthracite Boot Camp, in addition to my experience in the Corps, inspired a lifelong "Sense of Honor". The inspiration can and should surface not only in profound loyalty to country and family, but also in our professional public service to business clients and co-workers. The benefits received from such inspiration motivates the recipient to provide the highest level of service, resulting also in a high level of personal gratification. It should be obvious to most people that the overall Sense of Honor in our nation needs to be restored to the elevated level that once existed. We must focus diligently to follow laws, rules, and moral principles.

(2) FOCUSED DILIGENCE

One doesn't need to work in a coal mine to learn to work diligently; but it was that experience that helped guide me throughout life. I graduated from The University of Detroit's engineering school in 1967, worked for an Architectural and Engineering firm in Scranton for eight years, and then for the large utility that provides water and power to central Arizona, i.e., The Salt River Project(SRP). In 2003, I had an opportunity to retire from SRP with full benefits, after twenty-eight years of service. Two weeks after 'retirement' at age sixty-one, I interviewed with a large engineering consulting firm in Phoenix. I explained to the committee of three interviewers that I had been out of engineering and in positions of administrative management at SRP for the previous fifteen years; but would now like to return to my original career as a professional structural engineer. I was particularly attracted to the new era of computer design technology. I assured the interviewers that despite lacking recent technical design experience, I could do the work to their satisfaction. I sincerely wanted to get back into structural engineering and construction; however, without any such experience in the previous fifteen years, it was difficult to imagine that they would want to hire me. Therefore, as Nonno, Dad, and my Uncles had proposed to Barber Motors in Pittston in 1937, I proposed to my interviewers that I would be willing to work without a salary for a two months to demonstrate my 'focused diligence'. In response, the lead interviewer said, "*It's been my experience that when you pay nothing, you receive nothing in return. Therefore, we'll start you at a modest pay grade.*" He obviously was unaware of my extensive training in Anthracite Boot Camp. If he were aware, he would know there was no way he would "receive nothing in return" during that trial period. After my achievements in engineering over the past 17 years, including several technical design publications and job promotions, he now has a much better understanding. The experience made me ask myself, '*How can anyone be unemployed for a prolonged period of time if they truly want employment?*" The answer is they won't be, if they simply tell the employer they will initially work without pay, and then demonstrate very focused diligence in their work! In recent years, when asked if I plan to retire from work soon, I usually jest, "*I'm just warming up!*" To others I might respond, "*You call this* **WORK?**" All jesting aside, everyone knows that at times, office employment can be tedious, frustrating, challenging, and tiresome; but after my experiences in Anthracite Boot Camp, I suspect office professions shouldn't be considered "hard work". It certainly isn't like working in a four-foot high anthracite dog-hole. Let's just say that thanks to training in Anthracite Boot Camp, including intense instructions in the application of "Jinnegar", and the constant reminders to "Run, Don't Walk", I was inspired to provide focused and diligent professional service. Others can and should be similarly inspired by other means and methods available to them. Besides, there is always plenty of time available after evening dinner at home to e-mail friends, or to check the latest political and professional sports news.

(3) LEADERSHIP

Another lesson learned in Anthracite Boot Camp stemmed from Dad's obvious style of supervision and leadership. He started earlier and worked longer than those he supervised. He didn't dictate orders, and then retreat out of the mine. He led by example by working harder, and by offering assistance to each miner when that miner was faced with a difficult task. He very commonly demonstrated a strong friendship with the miners and their families that persisted at family picnics, 'prosciutto parties' at the dog-hole, and at the Italian American Citizen's Club. The following is an example of such leadership that I witnessed outside of Boot Camp. From 1968 to 1975, I was employed at an Architectural and Engineering firm in Scranton, Pennsylvania, and the CEO's particularly sensitive style of supervision and management was very reminiscent of Dad's. The CEO was Edward Loewe of Clarks Summit, Pennsylvania. In some of the many instances when I remained in my office well after 5:00 pm, Ed would slowly walk into my office with hands on hips, and sensitively ask the following sequence of questions:

"Lou, how are you?"

"What are you working on?"

"Lou, how is it going? Do you need any help?"

"How is your family? "

"Lou, why don't you go home and spend more time with your family?"

Granted, I was young and inexperienced at the time; but Ed's style set the ultimate example of professional, inspirational leadership. He fully empowered his experienced staff; but also toned it with frequent offers of guidance and assistance. The style can be applied and adjusted to all levels of staff experience. With that style, a team's quantity and quality of service will surely expand with continuous improvement. Dad's dialogue with the miners was a little rougher; but friendship, intent, attitude, and sincerity were the same as Ed's. I believe all supervisors and leaders should inspire proficient employees in a similar manner. Of course, the model of leadership for semi-proficient employees would be a little more direct.

(4) COLLABORATION

It almost goes without saying that the small group of coal miners working side by side in a treacherous underground chamber functioned as a team. Such teamwork was essential to their survival. However, Dad wasn't like the average football team coach, who calls plays and gives orders. When faced with difficult and dangerous underground tasks, Dad solicited and listened to the opinions of other miners. The miners communicated as a team inside and outside the mine, during and after their dangerous workday. In the search for continuous improvement, managers should solicit opinions from all team members, and not just departmental "quarterbacks" or "Captains". After all, the quarterback doesn't block, tackle, or run pass routes, and any indifference to those on the team who perform these critical functions can dampen their diligence. Opinions and opportunities for more efficient work processes and continuous improvement in quality and quantity should be solicited from everyone on the team who participates in fulfilling the team's mission. Such collaboration should be on-going as it is in a coal mine, and not just at annual functions or in annual surveys. In some professions, the constructive communication should also extend out to the suppliers and customers, and not just to the production team. The photo in Figure 13 has hung on my office wall for many years, not far from the chunk of anthracite on my bookshelf. At the instant the photo was snapped at the top of Mt. Suribachi on the Island of Iwo

Jima in February 1945, the "team" roared in unison: "**GUNG HO!**" The message is in a Chinese dialect, and originated when Marines served in China early in the twentieth century. Its' literal translation orders, "**WORK TOGETHER!**". There are a few officers and sergeants in the photo, but the majority are privates and corporals. It likely is the ultimate inspiration, resulting from an honorable team's focused diligence, to proudly demonstrate intense teamwork and "collaboration".

(5) DIPLOMACY: "DUCK A" VERSES "DUCK B"

It strikes me as very unusual that Dad could work so intensely focused; but yet, collaborate with his team so sensitively and diplomatically. Typically, one might expect that a person who is a human dynamo at daily physical labor, would be volcanic in their collaboration with others. However, Dad's "Putanna Concerts" were only directed at equipment that didn't function properly, and I usually was the only by-stander in the 'concert audience', or on the sidelines. A team leader or member can be honorable, diligent, and extremely focused; but totally unheeded, or fired, if their intensity is not under control. I have privately joked with a few hot-tempered friends to suggest they are like "Duck B", and need to be more like "Duck A". Leader "A" treats potentially hot, emotionally charged issues like "water off a duck's back". My sketch on my friend's office white board pictures a quacking Duck B with blue water puddled on its' back. Next to it, a sketch of Duck A pictures a happy-go-lucky duck with water running off its' back. When collaborating with his anthracite team, friends, or family, I guarantee Dad was naturally soft-spoken and diplomatic. In scene after scene in home videos, Dad is shown listening politely to family and friends, relaxed, and with arms folded. Most certainly, Dad was an absolute human dynamo at manual labor; but "Duck A" when collaborating with his miners and family. Figure 13 is an outstanding example of a

FIG. 13 — "GUNG HO!"

focused team's intense collaboration. "Duck B" is invaluable when attacking an enemy gun emplacement; but before providing professional public or personal services, all grenades, bayonets, and flame-throwers should be checked in with the receptionist at the office entrance.

BOOT CAMP SUMMARY

In summarizing 'Lessons Learned', some may ask, *"Well the 'lessons learned' sound like a great experience resulting from your background; but would they in fact mean anything to others of a totally different background?"* As mentioned earlier, one doesn't need to work in an anthracite mine or join the Marines to experience and apply the five 'Lessons Learned'. Isn't it obvious that anyone in every walk of life can make a conscientious effort to apply them without enlisting in Anthracite Boot Camp? Ultimately, the benefit of the 'lessons learned' is a positively inspired, professional and personal lifestyle. Anyone who has been around for the past six-plus decades can attest to the potential values of these benefits in reducing our current national trend toward 'scams', deteriorating public service, and illicit behavior. Society appears to have more 'free time' available, and isn't inclined to use it as constructively as was the ultimate necessity in the earlier decades of economic hardship summarized in the first three chapters of this book. History and current events suggest there is no guarantee that the previous "ultimate necessity" won't one day return.

Of course, the ultimate solution isn't as simple and straight-forward as I suggest. In a conversation that I had with Aunt Mary Dziuba before she passed away several years ago, she said to me, *"Your Dad taught you very well."* However, I will admit there have been times in recent years when some family and friends have suggested to me that Dad may have taught me 'too well'. According to them, one potential shortfall in my 'Lessons Learned' is that I should be spending less time at structural engineering design "work", and more time with my children and grandchildren. Unfortunately for me, that lesson wasn't covered in Anthracite or Marine Corps Boot Camp. However, it is an 'on-going battle' for which I plan to seek further training from my wife, three children, and five grandchildren. In the meantime, the five 'lessons learned', above, and particularly the childhood experience and memories of working at the mines with Dad, have been a life-long inspiration for me. It would be very difficult for me to trade them for any new inspiration that I may be offered. Nevertheless, I'm confident we will reach an amenable agreement soon at the end of our current battle, which otherwise, I'm very likely to lose. My "lost battle" can be interpreted by ABBA's 1976 heartfelt hit song, "**Fernando**". In it they very sensitively sing of the Mexican War battle they lost after crossing the Rio Grande, and then conclude with, "*But if I had to do it all again, I would, my friend, Fernando*". Besides, unknown to my family, it is mostly for their ultimate financial benefit that I continue to "work" diligently, though my loyalty is obviously transparent to them.

CONCLUSION

Any visitor to The Wyoming Valley in the anthracite region of Northeastern Pennsylvania can't help but notice the dozen or more tall, electric generating wind turbines that are now lined up along the mountaintop skyline on the east side of the Valley. Whenever I re-visit the Valley, the dominating sight of the rotating, giant steel propeller blades inspires me to recall my childhood training at anthracite dog-holes on Irish Hill, which is only a short distance west, and slightly downhill from those mountain-top turbines. The inspiration also guides me to re-visit the village of Old Boston, and some of the other former mining sites further down in the Valley where I worked with Dad sixty to seventy years ago. For the most part, the miners, mines, and coal breakers have passed on; however, the steel turbines tower over the towns and former mining villages in the Wyoming Valley where many thousands of hardened anthracite miners once persevered, served, and continue to be remembered as an inspiration for their descendants. Thus, the electric generating turbines currently serve as an 'Iwo Jima Flag-Raising' monument to those hard-working miners and their families, and the proud Anthracite Coal Mining Industry that the turbines eventually replaced. In a stoic but monolithic image, the mountain-top monument symbolically broadcasts an inspirational message out over the Valley, which emphatically advises:

GUNG-HO!

GLOSSARY AND PAGE INDEX OF MINING TERMS

BLACK DAMP: Carbon dioxide in the form of a thin vapor that replaces oxygen in the mine chamber and asphyxiates the miner. (Page 114)

BLACK LUNG: Lungs embedded with coal dust after years working underground. (Page 37)

BOND (STRIP-MINE): A financial bond of several thousand dollars, which the mine operator legally posts in the name of the landowner. The bond is returned after the operator restores the surface of the ground to its original condition, at the end of mining operations. (Page 59)

BONEY: The rock slate found embedded in a coal vein and considered an impurity that must be removed, or the weight of the coal will be docked by the weighmaster. (Page 59)

BOOTLEG: Coal that is illegally mined for individual household use or sold by the miner without a royalty payment to the owner of the mining rights. (Page 27)

BOTTLE COAL: Very hard anthracite that sounds like glass bottles when chunks bump together. (Page 83)

BREAKER: A large structure (Figure 2) in which mined coal is prepared for retail sales by bringing it to the top with a conveyor line, and dropping it from one level to the next so the coal is crushed, screened to various sizes, and silt is washed away. (Page 27)

CAP PIECE: Wood wedge hammered above a prop to wedge the prop between mine floor and roof, as shown in figure 12. (Page 63)

CHAMBER: Underground room where the coal has been extracted. (Page 1)

COLLIERY: A mine employing a large number of miners, and usually, the site of a breaker, also. (Page 28)

CUTTING COAL: The practice of drilling coal with a precision that makes it a marketable size and blasts it to the most convenient position to load or scoop without causing a roof collapse. (Page 66)

DEAD WORK: Work required to maintain the mine, other than mining coal. Examples are setting props, drilling a cut of coal, and gobbing rock. (Page 95)

DELAYS: Fuses set in sticks of dynamite to time detonations so that not all drill holes explode at the same time. (Page 66)

DOCK: Weighmaster's reduction in the true weight of a truckload of coal as a penalty for coal of lesser quality than the quality that prevailed when the original sales price was set. (Page 60)

DOGHOLE: Slang expression for a small underground mine employing few miners. (Preface)

EXPLODERS: Fuses set in sticks of dynamite to set off the explosion as soon as the electric switch is thrown in the shanty. (Page 66)

FACE: Wall of the vein to which mining has progressed and location where miners are working. (Page 62)

GANGWAY: The main tunnel where rails are in place for coal cars to be loaded and hoisted out to the tipple. (Page 98)

GOB: Waste area inside the mine chamber where boney or fallen roof rock is shoveled aside. (See "Dead Work")

MARY ANN: Slang for the equipment near a tipple that dumps mine cars full of rock into a truck or railroad car. (Page 99)

MUCKING: Moving water saturated soil or silt to get at the coal. (Page 87)

OUTCROP: The location where the deep vein of coal extends to the ground surface. (Preface)

PINCHED VEIN: The natural thickness of a vein of coal is geologically reduced so that the miners are forced to work under extremely cramped quarters until the vein eventually returns to its natural height. (Page 63)

PROPS: Wood logs cut from local forests, then cut to size in the mine, and wedged between mine floor and roof to prevent roof collapse after the coal is removed. (Page 47, also see Figure 12).

ROBBING PILLARS: Period near end of a mine's life when remaining columns of coal are removed in their entirety, or nearly so. (Page 94)

RIB: Walls of the coal vein at the sides of the tunnel or chamber. (Page 113, also see Figure 12).

ROLL: A geological anomaly in a vein of coal where it abruptly terminates and reappears again some short distance away. (Page 113)

ROYALTY: Payment per ton by the mining company to the legal owner of the mining rights to the coal mined. (Page 27)

SCABS: Slang expression given by miners to co-workers who continued mining coal after the majority of miners declared a strike for improved benefits. (Page 8)

SCOOP: Slang expression for the steel bucket that drags about one ton of coal out of the mine. (Page 43, also see Figure 7).

SHAKER: Mine system that slides coal out of the mine on a chute that rocks back and forth.(Page 58)

SOAPSTONE: The accumulation of a thin film of soapy silt on the rock surface of a mine's roof as water seeps along the roof from tiny cracks. (Page 87)

SETTLEMENT: Name given to a small, usually remote, community 100–150 years ago where miners and their families settled around a large mine or colliery. (Page 11)

SQUEEZE: Mine roof gradually settles as coal pillars are robbed or reduced in size. (Page 94)

STRIP MINE: Coal is mined by stripping away the overlaying soil and rock. (Page 59)

TAMPING BAGS: Round paper tubes filled with coal dust and inserted in a drill hole after sticks of dynamite were inserted. The bags force the detonated dynamite to explode laterally into the coal, instead of back out the drill hole. (Page 66)

TAMPING STICKS: Used to ram the tamping bags into the drill hole after the dynamite sticks had been inserted. (Page 66)

TIPPLE: A large wood structure (also called a "pocket") open at the top so coal cars on a sloping track could dump their loads, and trucks underneath could be loaded through a gate. Called "tipple" because in some variations, the coal cars were on horizontal tracks that could be tipped to dump their loads. (Page 29, also see Figure 3).

TOPPER: Miner who tops mine car or truck with chunks of anthracite to build up load carrying capacity of the mine car or truck. Often does so to also dress up the appearance of the coal's quality when it is delivered to the Breaker. (Page 100)

VEIN: A layer of coal, usually three to eight feet thick, and embedded between other layers of rock. (Page 1, also see Figure 12).

WEIGHMASTER: Technician at the breaker who manages the truck scale, reads the weight of the truck's load, applies any dockage, and issues a receipt to the driver. (Page 60)

X, Y, or Z LICENSE DUMP TRUCK: The first letter on the license plate, denoting official truck size and reference to its' legal wheel load weight limit. (Page 32, also see Figure 4).

INDEX OF TOWNS AND PLACES

INDEX TO NAMES

Uncles:

Others:

PAGE INDEX TO THE LIST OF FIGURES

OTHER READING

"I Remember Nonna", by August Carnevale,
published by iUniverse, 2007

"Anthracite Grade School on Irish Hill",
by Louis R. Scatena, Tate Publishing, 2015